Ukraine Love Affair

A True Story about Internet Romance

By

Calvin Parsons

Ukraine Love Affair

ISBN: 9781737024569
Copyright©2022 Calvin Parsons

Shades Creek Press, LLC

Printed in the United States of America

Cover Design by Calvin Parsons,
with final design by Natasha Walsh
Content Editing by Loraine Cabasa
All Photos of the Opera Hotel printed with permission
All other photos owned and printed by the author

All rights reserved. No part of this book may be used or reproduced in any manner, including Internet Usage, without express written consent of the author or publisher.

Disclaimer

This is a work of creative nonfiction. The events are portrayed to the best of Calvin Parson's memory. While all the stories in this book are true, some names and identifying details have been changed to protect the privacy of the people involved. Warning: Contains Graphic Adult Content.

*"I was lookin' for love in all the wrong places
Lookin' for love in too many faces"*

"Looking for Love"

Introduction

When my wife divorced me in 2015, I dialed in ludicrous mode. I spent two years sowing some pent-up wild oats and flying by the seat of my pants. I finally came in for a soft landing in Moscow, Russia in 2018. This book is the story of that journey.

There are events in our lives that will change us forever. Psychological trauma can cause us to do things we previously considered ridiculous. Some of the things I did are not the actions of a normal person. At the time, I wasn't normal. Sometimes the struggle back from outrageous fortune to normalcy can take us to places we have no business going. And, sometimes, we take shortcuts that are anything but short.

My story will take you to places no one should go. I went there and survived. But I should have never entered the swamp. Then, when I saw all of the dangers, I should have turned back. Ultimately, I decided to ignore the dangers and plunge forward, hoping conditions would improve. Yes, I survived, but I could have just as easily been consumed by the quagmire. I am fortunate.

Ladies and gentlemen, this is the Captain. There is some turbulence just ahead. Please return to your seats and fasten your seatbelts. Cabin service will be discontinued at this time. I am going to slightly alter our course to see if I can find some less turbulent conditions. In the meantime, please keep your seatbelts securely fastened. Thank you.

Foreword

Uber is the world's largest taxi company, but they don't own any cars. Airbnb is the largest hotel business on the planet, but they don't own a single hotel. I had not even heard of Airbnb a few years ago. Now I use the application regularly. The internet continues to change our lives in so many ways.

Most of us don't realize how the internet has changed dating and matchmaking. Most people don't care. But almost everyone will be looking for companionship and love at some point in their lives and now the internet is a viable option in that search.

A lot of people continue to just call a taxi. And most people still think using the internet for dating is "looking for love in all the wrong places." I believe that perception is beginning to change. I think more and more people will be using this method in the future.

One of the reasons I am writing this book is to provide some guidance through this very complicated and potentially dangerous process. I am hoping someone will learn from my experience. I am also writing it to gain a better understanding of this very complicated and controversial part of my life.

I am not a professional writer. I don't know the difference between a split infinitive and a dangling participle. Both terms sound mildly sexually suggestive to me. I am just a simple storyteller, and this is my story.

My story is true, but I made some assumptions that turned out to be wrong. I give my opinion and my opinion changed over time. Others will have conflicting opinions and they might be right.

It is not my objective to give specific advice. I simply tell a true story about success, hope, failure, despair, and survival. If you have ever been in love, you are likely familiar with these feelings. I hope you will learn something from my successes and my failures. And I hope I have learned something. But I am a slow learner.

Part One

Chapter One

My story is true. I have changed a few names but most of them are real. The places are real and so are the facts. But just because the story is true doesn't mean it's believable. I am reasonably certain you will not believe everything I have written. It will help immensely if you have been in love.

I was born on a 200-acre farm in northwest Florida. Floridians call this area "the Panhandle." Oddly, as a child, I never even wondered why. Years later it became obvious. A few years ago, I saw a political cartoon about Florida. It showed the penis shape that lies between the Atlantic Ocean and the Gulf of Mexico. The cartoon was captioned, "Electile Dysfunction."

My father was a man's man. I think he was a woman's man as well. He was handsome and quiet and almost everyone liked him. The only people who didn't like him were people who made the mistake of crossing him. He never started a fight, but he seldom avoided one either. He was also what some call an episodic alcoholic. He would go for months without a drink and then he would be drunk for a few days. I could look out the school bus window, see him on his tractor a quarter of a mile away, and tell if he was drinking. He was never violent when he was drinking. He just stayed away from the family until the episode was over. And we always welcomed him back with open arms. At least my brother and I did. Our mother was a different story altogether.

My family attended a very conservative Southern Baptist church about 300 yards from our house. Things like drinking and dancing were considered sinful. I didn't understand why my dad could continue to sin regularly. I was so damn naïve. My father was at Normandy. He wasn't there on the first day, but he was there. His infantry division made it to Paris before the war ended. His war experience coupled with his struggles through the Great Depression had changed him. He was just trying to survive. I would have done the same things he did. No, I would have done worse things.

Farming is hard work. But, since it doesn't take much brain power, there is a lot of time for conversation. My dad wasn't much of a talker. He gave me almost no advice. I was pretty much on my own. One exception was when I would ask for his help with a difficult situation in my life. He would listen very attentively to my entire story. Then, his usual response was, "Son, you traded for it." As a child, I never understood exactly what that meant. What had I traded for? Years later I realized he was saying I had brought my problems on myself. Something I had done had caused all of my difficulties. I had sewn some bad seed and now I was reaping the bad results.

The problems I brought on myself during the two years or so after my divorce in early 2015 were numerous. There were many times when I heard my father's words echoing in my head. "Son, you traded for it."

I loved and respected my father. I forgave him for everything he did and for everything he didn't do. I am including his photo in this book. That's him astride a Harley Davidson motorcycle somewhere in Belgium near the end of World War Two.

My father, somewhere in Belgium, near the end of World War Two

Chapter Two

A friendly divorce has to rank right up there with the world's greatest oxymorons. Even when the parties are relatively cooperative, it's highly unlikely that all of the issues can be resolved while maintaining a civil relationship. When most of the legal dust finally does begin to settle, there are still practical issues that must be addressed. One of those issues is simply finding a place to live. We know the perils of making critical decisions while amid emotional turmoil, but some things just can't wait.

My friends call me a handyman. A jealous husband once called me "Bob Fucking Vila." And I was only repairing his wife's kitchen sink.

After the divorce, I bought a house in the same neighborhood because my grandson liked to fish in the lake there. For the next couple of months, I was busy trying to make my new house a home. I have no clue why that included installing a whole-house emergency generator, but it made perfect sense at the time. And I don't mean calling the experts for the installation. I mean ordering the generator online, installing the plumbing and electrical wiring, and getting it all up and running. During that period, the last thing on my mind was dating. Of course, some people are well into the social scene before finalizing the divorce. I was not one of those people.

For me, the first desire was certainly not sexual. I just wanted to go out to a nice restaurant and have some good food and wine. But I just couldn't imagine going out alone as being much fun.

So, I began thinking of some friends I might call. I came up with a list of a half dozen candidates. One of those candidates was a much younger woman I had recently met while looking for a retirement community for my mother. I thought we had a connection, and she was a very attractive lady. As it turned out I must have been wrong about the connection. She didn't even return my call. Well, so much for younger women.

Most of the women on my shortlist were closer to my age. After all, I wasn't looking to hook up; I was just looking for a dinner companion. When I finally contacted some of the women on my list, I discovered that my divorced friends were not so much interested in the dating scene. Even when I explained the "it's just dinner" concept, they didn't think it was worth the time and effort. And the two widows I called were still madly in love with their deceased husbands. I pretty much struck out. By this time, I was getting a little desperate and my ego was somewhat bruised. I should mention here that patience is not one of my strengths—at least that's what some people say.

For an older man, I consider myself relatively up to speed in the electronic age. I have been a very active eBay member since 1998, the year the business was founded. My username is since90eight. I have completed more than 500 transactions and I have 100% positive feedback. If you want to sell something, there is no better way to get your product noticed. If the internet works for motorcycles and cars, why wouldn't it work for people? That is the very simple reason I turned to internet dating. I should add by this time my anxiety and desperation had brought sex into the equation. I was still looking for a dinner companion, but I also just needed a woman.

So, I picked out a couple of the popular dating websites and began working on a profile. I posted some very generic information in my profile, and I used iPhone photos that weren't exactly made for the purpose. I took a photo in a t-shirt in front of my bathroom mirror. I posted the photo and immediately began to get hits. I remember thinking how easy this was.

It quickly became obvious that most of the women were on these sites to chat. Just chat, nothing more. They might eventually decide to meet someone, but it would be somewhere down the road.

Chapter Three

I had been on these popular sites for a few days. I chatted with several interesting ladies. At least I assumed they were ladies. I have since concluded that the industry is replete with men in cubicles with a computer, an internet connection, and some pictures of beautiful women. It is so simple. Anyone can do it. This is one of the huge pitfalls of internet dating. After a while, you get a distinct feeling when it's happening. In the beginning, you don't have a clue.

It didn't take long to get comfortable with the chatting. Then something strange happened. I received a chat message from an attractive young woman who lived in Poplarville, Mississippi. Heather was a nursing student at a local junior college there. She told me she had seen my profile and was interested in meeting me. That was uncharted territory. I saw her age in her profile and told her she was too young for me. I even asked if she had noticed my age in my profile. She told me age meant absolutely nothing to her. I think her phrase was, "Age is just a number," which of course is total bullshit.

I told Heather she was too far away, but I would be happy to meet her sometime when she was closer to me. I was still in the chatting mode. Heather wasn't. She said she wanted to meet me today. The game had just changed in one hour.

We exchanged contact information and she began to text me. I began to retreat to familiar territory. I told her I could not come to Mississippi. She then told me she had transportation and would drive to Birmingham and would meet me at my house. I didn't believe her. She was 23 years old. She didn't know me from Adam, as they say. Calling her bluff, I told her to come on. I then went out to eat dinner with a friend. A couple of hours later, while I was sitting at the bar at Chuck's Fish, Heather called me on my cellphone. She told me she was having car trouble and had stopped at an interchange on I-59 near Hattiesburg, Mississippi. She asked me what she should do. I told her to call a wrecker. She said she had no money for a wrecker. I'm new at this but her scheme was becoming clearer by the minute.

    Heather proposed a new plan for our meeting. She suggested I come to Hattiesburg, pick her up and the two of us go to New Orleans for the weekend. I said, "Heather, I like the idea sweetheart, but I've had two drinks and there is no way in hell I can drive to Hattiesburg, Mississippi." And, it was true, I did like the idea. She was young and beautiful. I was old and horny. It was a match made in Heaven. She told me she was stranded in Hattiesburg. I said, "You certainly are and I'm sorry." I told her goodbye, ended the call, and ate dinner.

    At about the end of dinner, Heather appeared on my cellphone. She had a new plan. She was having her Hummer towed back to Poplarville. She asked me to pay the wrecker bill. Now, this was becoming obvious. It was a simple scam. I told her there was no way I was sending her money for the wrecker bill or anything else. If I had only remembered this response, it would have saved me a lot of money in the future. Then Heather went to plan C. Or was it Plan D? I had lost count by now. She suggested I come down to Poplarville the next day, help her with the wrecker bill, and then the two of us go to New Orleans for a couple of days.

What happened next was the result of alcohol and desperation in just the right combination. I agreed. What's the worst thing that could happen? I drive to Mississippi for nothing, right? Well, wrong, actually. The worst thing that could happen was much worse than that. But by now this thing had taken on a life of its own. It was an adventure. I just had to know how it might end. I have since learned this is a weakness.

Early Friday morning I headed to Mississippi. Optimistically, I stopped by CVS for supplies. But I wasn't as confident as the night before for some reason. Even now I'm wondering if alcohol might have played a larger role in all of this than I thought. Don't laugh. It's a very legitimate question.

As I was driving through Meridian, I revisited the worst-case scenarios. There were a lot of possibilities. And these possibilities are what made what I was doing so dangerous. It also made it exciting. One such possibility is I pull up to her house, walk up to her door, and her husband meets me with a gun in his hand. Unlikely, you are thinking. Think again.

But that didn't happen. When I was twenty miles out, I called her and told her I would not be getting out of my vehicle. I apologized for not being a gentleman. She understood. I instructed her to be outside by the street with her bag. I also told her I had a loaded .38 Smith and Wesson revolver on the seat beside me. I know this sounds theatrical, but it is the truth. I tell her if she is afraid of guns, she can still change her mind. She wasn't afraid of guns.

As I pulled into the apartment complex, I saw her standing by the curb beside her little carry-on bag.

She was young and beautiful. The apartment complex was neither.

I met Heather on a website called Seeking Arrangement. It is one of the most popular sugar daddy/sugar baby sites on the internet. The site's primary purpose is to put two desperate people together. Men like me are desperate for obvious reasons. Women are desperate for various reasons too.

For example, they might have family issues. They might just want to be treated nicely for a change. By far the most common reason is they need money. It might be because their husband left them with children to feed. It might be that they can't make the car or rent payment. They might be unemployed. In Heather's case, it was her nursing education. She was one quarter from graduating and she was hell-bent and determined to finish. I admired her for that.

Heather knew I was nervous. I had made that abundantly clear. She quickly got into my car and I immediately exited the property. Or is it poverty. She needed a cigarette—yes, I get the irony; she is a nurse who smokes a little. I told her she couldn't smoke in the car.

I paid the wrecker bill directly to the owner of the wrecker. The drive from Poplarville to New Orleans was relatively short and uneventful. We checked into the Hotel Monteleone on Royal Street. It has been said that the French Quarter begins in the lobby of Hotel Monteleone. It has been there since 1886. It is one of my favorite hotels in the world. Heather and I had a drink at the lobby carousel bar. She told me a little about herself. I think some of it was even true. She was hungry so we walked down Bourbon Street and found a little corner café that wasn't too crowded. We had some good wine and some great Cajun food. We were back at the hotel by 10:00 p.m.

I had not seen a young woman's near-perfect body for a long time. Hers were extraordinary. She was uninhibited. This wasn't just an arrangement. She wanted to have sex. I was so excited I forgot about the condom. It wasn't because I was in a hurry. I had determined that I would take my time from this point forward in my sex life. I was going to stop and smell the roses, as it were. My looking at her naked body and taking my time only raised her arousal. After just a few minutes there was no stopping her.

After we were done, I noticed there was some blood on the white sheets. Not a huge amount like in the horse head scene in the first *Godfather* movie, but not just a spot or two either. I asked Heather if she was on her period. She said no but she had not had sex in two years, and she felt like a virgin. I told her how sorry I was for not being more careful. She said, "I promise you the pleasure was worth the pain." That's when I awarded her the Oscar for best supporting actress.

It was nice being in bed with a woman with a beautiful warm body—especially a body that belongs to someone who has passed organic chemistry. I slept like a baby. Early the next morning her cellphone rang. Her mother, who lived near her in Poplarville, had had a heart attack and been taken to the hospital. Now, this might sound like an unusual and unlikely event, but the common thread running through these women is that the vast majority are drama queens. And most of the drama is real.

Heather asked me what she should do. There was no doubt in my mind. We packed our bags and headed north to Mississippi. On the way to Poplarville, she asked me to take her directly to the hospital. This was perfect for me. A hospital is a public place. I was back in the cautious mode. However, just before we got to the hospital, she asked me to stop by and pick up her brother on the way. She made it sound so very reasonable. It likely was reasonable. But there was no way in Hell a stranger was getting his ass in the seat behind me. I told her as much. I said those exact words. She got a little upset and told me to take her to her uncle's house. I then called one of my best friends and asked him to stay on the phone with me for a few minutes. I also took my .38 out of the center console.

We drove down a desolate street. Most of the houses were vacant. There were dogs roaming around. The area was a mess. A man was sitting on a front porch. It was a dead-end street. I stopped the car about a hundred yards from the house. Heather told me the man was her uncle and everything was fine. I told her to get out of the car and take her bag with her. She thought I was crazy. She was right.

Heather called me a couple of times during the next few weeks. One time she needed money. One time she just wanted to know how I was doing. I couldn't help but think how being intimate with someone ties the two of you together forever. It's a very fine thread in some cases, but it's always there.

Chapter Four

When I returned home from Mississippi, I began a long period of internet dating that involved more than 30 women. The youngest was 19 and the oldest was 57. Most of these women I saw once or twice. A few of them were around, off and on, for months. A couple of weeks after the New Orleans adventure I received a message on the Seeking Arrangement website from Shanda. She had seen my profile and picture and wanted to meet. While we messaged on the site, I looked at her picture and profile there. She was very attractive. She asked if she could call me. This was very unusual. Normally the site messaging goes on for a while, then you text for a while, and eventually, you might talk on the phone. But I told her it was fine if she called me. I sent her my cellphone number and waited. She called me in five minutes.

When I had a problem pronouncing her name she told me, "It's Shanda, as in chandelier." She quickly asked if I would like to meet her for dinner. I told her I would be happy to meet her for dinner sometime. She said, "Great, I'm on Highway 280, meet me at Chuck's Fish in 30 minutes." Then she quickly added, "But there will be no sex on the first date." It had not even crossed my mind there would be sex on the first date. I'm not saying it's a bad idea, I'm just saying it didn't cross my mind.

I eat at Chuck's Fish often. It is convenient to where I live, and the fresh seafood is great. I put a sports coat on over my jeans and head out to Chuck's.

Shanda and I had a nice meal and shared a bottle of good white French Burgundy. She told me a little about herself. I thought there might be a connection there. If there isn't some chemistry between two people, an arrangement is just not worth the time and effort. At the end of the meal, she asked me if Chuck's had any good dessert. I told her the white chocolate bread pudding was excellent. She motioned to our waiter who came directly over. She said to him, "Please bring us an order of the white chocolate bread pudding to go." I asked her where we were going. She said, "We are going to your house."

At this point, I vividly recall making a dumb comment. I said, "Shanda, I thought you said there would be no sex on the first date."

She replied, "We aren't going to have sex. I just want to see where you live."

Shanda left her car at Chuck's. We were at my house in ten minutes. The bread pudding was great, as usual. I opened a bottle of the same wine we had had at Chuck's. We talked for an hour or so. I think we went upstairs to bed around 10:30. At 1:00 a.m. I asked her if she would like to get some sleep. Her reply was, "I would rather fuck if it's okay with you." Most people will think I'm exaggerating or bragging here. Neither is the case. Marathon sex doesn't happen to me often, but if everything is just right, it can happen. And everything was just right. I asked her if I could take a tasteful picture of her beautiful body. She didn't mind the picture and she didn't mind me slowing down to smell the roses either. Shanda was in her mid-thirties at the time. I was getting addicted to young bodies. I mean truly addicted.

A few days after that first date, Shanda and I went on a beach trip to Destin, Florida. Again, the sex was terrific. I began to think I could be happy with this woman. I could stop this crazy internet dating early. There were just two little problems with my thinking. First, the closer I got to Shanda, the further she pulled away. She thought I might be falling in love with her; she wasn't ready for that. And second, she wanted the finer things of life. I was giving her a weekly allowance, but she wanted more.

I think our relationship lasted about a month. She asked me to meet her for lunch on a beautiful early spring day in Birmingham. I knew she had something to tell me. There on a park bench she told me she had to move on. And just like that, it was over. My heart wasn't broken but losing Shanda so quickly was a painful shock.

Chapter Five

Early on, I began establishing some rules about my internet dating program. Most of these rules were usually the result of a really bad experience. The first rule I initiated was simple and effective. I decided I would never reach out to any woman on any website.

I would simply put my honest pictures and profile out there and wait. My theory was I could save a lot of time and embarrassment by not making the first contact. I knew the vast majority of women would simply pass when they saw my age and pictures.

A picture of a beautiful woman in Tuscaloosa had captured my attention, but I resisted the temptation to send her a message. Then, she made me one of her favorites and I couldn't resist. But I was very careful to make it easy for her to decline. I told her I was too old for her and thanked her for her attention. I told her I was flattered.

Her response was, "Are you kidding me? I would be happy to meet you anytime. Why don't you come down here and take me to dinner this evening?" It was around 4:00 p.m. She told me she could be ready by 6:30 p.m.

I asked her how she felt about having dinner at the Cypress Inn Restaurant in Tuscaloosa. The restaurant is located on the Warrior River and the food is good. She said that would be great.

April was 37 years old. Her pictures on the website were beautiful. I didn't believe they were real. I just had to see for myself. Curiosity was beginning to rear its ugly head. And it damn near killed the cat.

All of our communications had been by text. Then April suggested we talk on the phone. I gave her my cellphone number and she called me immediately. We firmed up our dinner plans. Then she gave me the now-familiar line, "There will be no sex on our first date." I believed her.

I don't know exactly what I was expecting when I arrived in Tuscaloosa, but it wasn't the girl in the site photos. I was wrong. When she came to the door I was immediately shocked at her beauty. And she was about half-dressed. She quickly asked me to come in while she finished dressing. Her garage apartment was small. She came in and out of the living room holding up various pieces of clothing and asking my opinion. I don't remember any of the clothes.

When she was finally dressed, she suggested we go pick up some wine and takeout and bring it back to her apartment. That suited me just fine. We went to Publix and picked up a few groceries and some salad and wine for dinner. She opened a bottle of the wine and poured two big glasses. After two of these, I told her I needed to find a hotel room for the night because I wasn't going to drive back to Birmingham after drinking so much wine. She said, "Don't be silly, you are staying here." I just about passed out.

We talked for a long time and drank more wine. I learned that April is a freelance model. I wasn't surprised. She is one of those sexy women who hold up lap signs at dirt bike races. I kept several of her professional pictures on my cellphone for a long time. Every time I looked at them, I was amazed at her beauty.

The very beautiful and very crazy woman from Tuscaloosa

We drank two bottles of wine with dinner. Then we went to bed. Again, I forced myself to slow down and keep my eyes open. She was proud of her body and was not the least bit intimidated by my staring. It turned her on. It was just wonderful.

Then around 1:30 a.m., April got out of bed. I asked her if anything was wrong. She told me she wanted some more wine. I told her I wasn't going out drunk at this time of night to look for more wine. She said, "That won't be necessary. I will call a good friend and tell him to go pick up a bottle for us." Even in my inebriated condition, I could see red flags waving everywhere. I told her I wasn't comfortable with her plan. She explained that he was just a friend who would do anything for her. I completely understood that.

Thirty minutes later there was a soft knock on the door. I had no idea what was about to happen. I did know that most of the things that were likely to happen were bad. None of this was making any sense to me. Who would ask someone to get out of bed in the middle of the night just to go pick up a bottle of wine?

I wasn't prepared for anything bad. My .38 was in the car and I was naked. But I knew I wasn't going to be horizontal when this guy came in, so I grabbed my jeans and put them on as April answered the door.

A small, older, meek, and mild guy stuck his head and a bottle of wine in the door. April gave him twenty dollars, thanked him, and he quickly left. I had forgotten to breathe for a while. I let out an audible breath. She just laughed.

April drank the wine and listened to some wild music on the television. It was then about 2:30 a.m. She finally got back in bed around 3:00 a.m. When we woke up it was raining. It was Sunday morning, and I could think of no place I'd rather be than right there in that bed with April. She got up and went to the kitchen. I thought we were about to have some breakfast. I got out of bed and walked into the kitchen. She was standing there in almost nothing and she was pouring Grey Goose into a large glass. She added just enough cranberry juice to the vodka to give it a very light pink tint.

I turned around and went back into the living room. I began putting my clothes on. She told me she wanted me to stay and spend the day with her. I told her I had to get back to Birmingham. I didn't say anything about the vodka, but she knew what I was thinking. We argued about her drinking and my leaving. For the first time, she raised her voice. She told me not to be so judgmental. She was correct; I had no right. The vodka drink was almost gone. I kissed her goodbye and headed back home.

April called me every day for the next week or so. I should have ended it but I simply couldn't get her beauty out of my mind. When I began to think I was wrong about her beauty, I just looked at her pictures and saw I was right. I knew I didn't want to deal with her issues, but I just couldn't pull the trigger on leaving her for good.

About three weeks after I left April in Tuscaloosa, she called me on my cellphone. She was crying. She was in Orlando, Florida. Some guy had sent his airplane to pick her up in Tuscaloosa and take her to Orlando. They had gotten along well in the beginning. She had met his kids. All of them had gone out to eat at a nice restaurant in Orlando. She told me the guy had gone postal in the restaurant for no reason.
What likely happened is that she had gotten drunk and made a fool of herself in front of the children and the guy just reacted. But I couldn't be sure it was all her fault. In any event, he had put her on the street. He

must have given her some money for one night in a motel.

April told me to get in my car and come to Orlando to get her. She had almost no money and was likely hung over. I checked the distance to Orlando on my cellphone. It's a long way from Birmingham. Then I asked her how far it was to the bus station. Miraculously, she said two blocks. I told her I would buy her a bus ticket to Tuscaloosa online. She wasn't happy. I purchased the ticket and called her back. I told her to be at the bus station at 6:00 a.m. She thanked me and told me I was the only friend she had.

April called me crying at 6:15 the next morning. She had overslept. Or she had passed out. The bus was leaving in 20 minutes, and she was still in the motel room. I told her to get her ass to the bus station. I told her the bus might be late. The bus was a few minutes late and she got to the station with no time to spare.

When the bus arrived in Tallahassee, April called me and asked me to meet her at the bus station in Birmingham because there was a three-hour layover. I agreed to pick her up and drive her to Tuscaloosa. She said she had been missing me. She told me again that I was her only friend. She wanted to see me. I looked at her pictures again. I called her back and suggested I meet her in Montgomery, Alabama. We could go to the beach for a few days. She was so happy that she started crying again.

I went online to Hotels.com and booked a little houseboat on the harbor in Destin, Florida for four days. I headed to Montgomery to meet her. The bus was late, but she finally arrived. I put her bag in the trunk of the car and we headed south on I-65. About an hour into the drive to Destin I asked her how she liked riding the bus. She asked me if I was making fun of her. I told her I was just making conversation. We argued. She screamed. That's when I should have turned the car around and headed north to Tuscaloosa. I recalled her stressful experience, thought about her pictures again, and apologized. I don't recall what I apologized for.

We arrived at the houseboat around 10:00 p.m. I had packed a bottle of the good French white, burgundy. I opened the bottle. April drank most of it while I was out for thirty minutes, picking up some seafood near the docks. I returned with shrimp and four margaritas. She drank both of hers quickly. Then she asked if I had a cigarette lighter. I told her it was a nonsmoking room and there was a $500 fine for smoking on the houseboat. She said she didn't care. She went out to find a lighter. In thirty minutes, she came back and came very close to falling into the water getting onto the houseboat. I could see something really bad happening here.

It was around 1:00 a.m. when she managed to get inside. She was not happy. She was drunk and wanted to fight. I told her I would sleep on the sofa, and we would get some sleep, and then start over in the morning. I was tired and I had had too much to drink. She then told me she wasn't sleeping alone. She was screaming again.

I began cleaning up the kitchen. I could hear her talking to me, but I didn't care what she was saying. My mind was made up. When the place was reasonably clean, I put my clothes in my suitcase and told her to get her shit together. She asked where we were going.

I said, "Tuscaloosa." She told me she wasn't going to Tuscaloosa. I said, "That's fine with me. Stay here, we have the place for four days." I picked up my suitcase and headed for my car. Ten minutes later, she got in the car with me. It was about 2:00 a.m. when we crossed the Destin Bay Bridge heading north.

April screamed almost continuously for about thirty minutes. She called me some very interesting names. Most of them hit home, especially the ones about my age. After she tired of screaming, she turned on her cellphone music at full volume. I am not a fan of rap music and I asked her to please turn the volume down. She told me to fuck off.

It was early March. The outside temperature was unusually cold, so I turned on my seat heater and let all of the windows down. It was freezing in the car. She asked me to please raise the windows. I agreed to raise the windows when she turned down the music. She refused. This was good because the cold air was sobering me up and keeping me awake. It was about 3:30 a.m. The music finally stopped. Her battery was dead. She was asleep.

When we were about thirty minutes south of Montgomery, April woke up and asked me to stop and let her smoke a cigarette. I said no. Just north of Montgomery, in Prattville, she told me she had to pee. I needed to get some gas. While I was pumping the gas, she smoked a cigarette. This was a wonderful opportunity to leave her ass right there. I wanted to, but for some reason, I just couldn't.

During the trip to Tuscaloosa, I counted the mile markers and kept reminding myself that this is my fault, not hers. I heard my father say, "You traded for it son."

When we were about five minutes from April's apartment, she asked me in the sweetest voice if I would mind stopping and getting her a soft drink. I didn't even acknowledge the question. When we arrived at her apartment, I took her bag out of the back seat and sat it on the driveway. Without a word I got back in my car and left. I did look back to see her carrying her bag upstairs to her apartment. When I was at the entrance to I-20/I-59 toward Birmingham the sun was coming up in my face. It hurt my eyes, but I knew I had survived the ordeal and I was almost home.

Chapter Six

As I have said, desperation was the common thread running through the internet dating process. I'm not going to go into every desperate situation I encountered. It's just too damn depressing. But, as an example, I will tell you about Raven.

Raven lives in Birmingham. She was 27 years old in 2015. She has two beautiful, smart young children. Her husband left her and she had to find a place to live quickly. She didn't want to move her kids out of the school district, but it was difficult finding a place. She had finally found an apartment, but it was in a less than desirable area of town. She was going through a difficult divorce. I honestly don't know how she functioned with all of the pressure. But she is a mother, and a mother will do whatever it takes.

Raven messaged me on the site, and we quickly moved to texting. She made it clear that she wanted an arrangement because she was in bad financial condition. She wanted to meet me immediately, so, I met her at a little sidewalk café near my house. We had a glass of wine and chatted for an hour.

Yes, Raven is beautiful. She is also exotic. She is from a mixed marriage, and she just happened to get the right DNA from both races. She had the biggest, darkest eyes I had ever seen. I hate to sound like an opportunist, but I could not wait to see her naked body, so I asked her if she wanted to come to my house which was only four blocks away. She agreed.

I poured her a glass of wine, and we discussed our potential arrangement. She told me how much money she needed every month to balance her budget. She was working but her income was about half of what she needed. I agreed to help her and we settled on a monthly amount. She asked me if I wanted to have sex with her. My answer was the same as any other red-blooded American male. Yes! Please. But when we got in bed, she was not ready. She would have done it but it just wasn't the right time. She wanted to be held and comforted. And I was happy to do that, but it certainly wasn't comforting for me. Raven had rather large breasts. They were a little large for my taste, but I adapted to them quickly. Her nipples were unusually large and dark, and they were erect. I finally gave her my very best oral sex routine and I could tell she had finally relaxed. I had not. But there was no intercourse and she thanked me for being so understanding. You are certainly fucking welcome, sweetheart.

I had agreed to give Raven a $1,500 monthly allowance. I gave her the first installment immediately. Her rent was due, along with the usual deposits. Two days later she called me and told me she needed an additional $1,100. I asked why she needed the money. She told me she had borrowed her rent money from her sister, and she had to pay her back immediately. I told her that she should have informed me about this before I gave her the $1,500. We argued and it appeared the arrangement would be over before it had begun.

I gave her the $1,100, but that initial disagreement affected our relationship for the two or three months we were together.

Raven was stressed out. Who wouldn't be? I suggested she ask her mother to keep the kids for a couple of days so we could take a short beach trip. She needed to get away from it all if just for a couple of days, and I wanted her to relax and let our relationship begin to happen.

The drive to the beach was fun. Raven was beautiful, she smelled good, and she was in a good mood. We listened to music on Pandora and the time flew by. When we got to Destin we checked into the hotel and then went directly to the beach. It was a weekday and there weren't many people on the beach. The ones who were there were looking at Raven like she was the Girl from Ipanema.

We ate dinner at a little place on the beach. The seafood in Destin is good just about everywhere. It has to be to compete with the other great restaurants there. But this food was unusually good. And the margaritas were even better. Things were looking up. Life was good.

We stayed at the beach until after sundown, but it was getting cool quickly, so we went to our room. We took a shower and got in the bed. She wanted to watch television. It was obvious that sex was not on the menu.

I want to make it clear that I am not interested in any kind of sex unless the woman is into it. It was apparent that Raven was not into it. It was beginning to become an issue. I could understand her being uptight at home, but this wasn't home. It was the fucking beach.

She wasn't in the mood, and she wasn't going to get in the mood. This wasn't my wife who had had a bad day. This was a woman with whom I had an arrangement and I had more than held up my end of the bargain. Raven had no intention of holding up her end. It was a shame. She was so damn sexy and so cold. That's not a good combination for me, so, I moved to the sofa and eventually went to sleep.

When we got up the next morning we argued. I was beginning to think Destin might not be the best place to bring women. My recent experiences here had been awful. I suggested we go home. She agreed. She insisted I take her to the bus station. That made absolutely no sense to me. I was driving back to Birmingham, and she lived in Birmingham. We would arrive about three hours before the bus. But she just didn't want to be in the car with me for five hours. She threatened to call the police and tell them she had been kidnapped. I was beginning to wonder if all women were crazy or was I the common denominator.

Raven finally settled down and we drove to Birmingham. It wasn't as much fun as the trip down. On the way home, she called her brother and told him how I had treated her. He was going to meet us at her apartment. When we were near her place, I called a good friend and asked him to stay on the phone with me for a while. I gave him the address of the apartment and other information. I was just being cautious, but it pissed off Raven.

When we arrived at her apartment, there was no confrontation. I hung up the phone. We quickly unloaded her bags and I left. We continued the arrangement for a few more weeks. During this time, I met her kids and we met for lunch or dinner. There was a little sex but it was nothing special. I know I helped her through a very tough time, and I don't regret the help I gave her and her kids. I certainly do regret not being able to make the arrangement work. She just wasn't ready for an arrangement, and I was not a patient man.

Raven and I are still friends. She recently called me after more than a year. She wanted to meet me for lunch at Seasons 52. I agreed. She later texted me and told me she would be dressed in her gym attire. I told her I would meet her at McDonald's. She told me she would be pretty enough for Seasons 52. She certainly was. When I arrived, she was sitting at an outside table on the patio. She was wearing a white Nike baseball cap. She was even more beautiful than I remembered, but my first thought was what a fucking shame.

While we were eating, she told me she was making a lot of money on an internet cam-sex site. She was making so much money that she had moved into a nice house in the same area. It was in a much nicer neighborhood.

I told Raven I had spent the past five weeks in Mexico. She said, "I want you to take me to Mexico." I asked when she wanted to go. She said, "Right away."

I don't know about Mexico. You can drive back from Destin but it's a little more difficult to get home from Cancun. She told me she wasn't ready for me earlier, but she wanted to be with me now. She wanted to show me how much she appreciated my help when she needed it the most. I'm still thinking about it. Something tells me I might need to brush up on my Spanish.

Chapter Seven

My mother lived in Calera, Alabama, until she died on March 22, 2016. She was 93. I spent a good bit of time with her during her last few months. She was surprisingly sharp right up to within a few days of her death. A few months before she died, I had been trying to get her to agree to go to an assisted living facility. She had even agreed to look at a couple. On one visit I finally insisted she start getting ready to move. She quietly asked me to hand her the phone. She immediately dialed the Calera Police Department from memory. She told the dispatcher her son was trying to throw her out of her house.

After my divorce, my mother would regularly ask me about my love life. I don't know why she found it so interesting. I always thought it was a little weird. We talked about it often. Of course, I only gave her the edited version.

My mother always questioned my internet dating method. She would ask me questions like, "Son, why don't you look for some nice woman at Walmart?" She didn't understand the internet, and she must not have noticed that the average Walmart woman weighs in at around 200 pounds. But weight and ugliness aren't my only issues with the Walmart method. The biggest problem is simple math. You might find a prospect or two on a visit to Walmart. On the internet, you can see hundreds at a time.

Anita lived next door to my mother in Calera. I think she still lives there. Mother talked about her often. It became obvious that she was trying to see if I would be interested in dating her. When I didn't take the bait, she asked me directly if I would be interested in dating Anita. I finally told mother I would ask Anita out if she would call her first and see if she might be interested in me. I know this is a little unusual, but I was just buying time and I thought that would be the end of it.

Within a couple of weeks, my mother called and told me she had talked with Anita, and she was interested in talking with me. Mother told Anita that I would call her.

I think I had met Anita a few years before at my mother's house. She is an attractive blonde woman in her mid-fifties. She is often outside working in her immaculate yard. She is slim and takes good care of herself—that is a little unusual for American women. Anita was, theoretically, ideal. Well, except for the fact that she is a member of some fundamentalist Christian church in Shelby County, Alabama. Mother had told me Anita was very active in her church and I should be respectful of her religious beliefs if I was interested in exploring a relationship with her. I didn't see a major problem with being respectful. I have a lot of religious friends. And, after all, I do live in the heart of the Bible Belt.

When I called Anita, she seemed rather shy and nervous. This was a new experience. I hadn't talked with a shy and nervous woman in years. I didn't know they still existed. However, after a few minutes, she relaxed, and we had a good conversation about things in general. I told her my mother was trying her hand at matchmaking and Anita agreed. We talked about my mother for a little while. Then I asked her if she would like to go out to dinner with me. She said yes immediately. We set a date and said our goodbyes.

When I called a few days later to confirm our date, I was surprised Anita brought up her religious beliefs. When she asked me where I went to church, I thought, well, this is the end of this. I was honest with her. I told her I was having some serious issues with religion. Then she asked me the acid test question, "Do you believe in God?"

I asked, "Which one?"

She didn't see the humor in my little joke. I told her candidly that I was agnostic. I explained that it simply meant I didn't know if there was a God or not. She was shocked. I visualized her there with the phone in her hand and her mouth open. I told her I completely understood if my lack of religious conviction was a deal-breaker for her. She said, "I still would like to go out to dinner with you." I was thinking that dinner was going to be an evangelical experience. Anita was going to try to save my soul.

There aren't any good restaurants in Calera, so, I drove the forty- five minutes down there, picked up Anita, and drove back to Chuck's Fish. We had a great seafood dinner. She drank two or three glasses of the magic white wine. I couldn't help but think this was a little strange. She liked the food at Chuck's as much as I did. She had the sautéed snapper. She couldn't believe how good it was.

We arrived at the restaurant around 7:15 p.m. By 8:45 we had finished dinner. When we got into the car, she asked me where I lived. I remember thinking how familiar this was beginning to sound. There was good magic at Chuck's and bad magic at Destin. I told her where I lived and that we would be going within five minutes of my house on our way back to her house. She said, "Why don't you take me there so I will know where you live?" This was totally unexpected.

I just replied, "I would be happy to do that."

I opened a bottle of the familiar white French Burgundy. This was the same wine we drank at Chuck's. I was thinking there must be something in this wine that makes people less inhibited. Well, yes there is; it's called alcohol.

Anita drank two more glasses of the wine. And then she wanted to talk about God again. I suggested we talk about something else, but she insisted. So, we had the usual conversation where the believer uses the Bible to prove the Bible. I think it's called circuitous logic. I'm not certain what it's called but I know it's ridiculous.

Anita was surprised that a reasonably intelligent person could have serious questions about God's existence. Unlike most people, she wasn't angry or defensive. She was just totally shocked. Then she told me a couple of mildly suggestive sexual jokes. Not dirty jokes by any means, they were just suggestive. If I was going to make a move, the time was now.

I likely will never know why I didn't make that move. I almost always do. Hell, I make the move sometimes even when there is no invitation. But I just couldn't do it. Maybe it was because I had counted the glasses of wine she had consumed. Maybe I respected her religious beliefs too much. Maybe I was wondering what my mother would think.

Whatever the reason, I knew for a fact my next move could be the turning point in our short relationship. Then I said, "Anita, it's a long way to Calera and back. I think we need to get going."

That splash of cold water shocked both of us. I couldn't believe I had said it. She was embarrassed. She had come to my house on our first date. She had gotten very comfortable and had let her hair down in my living room. My announcement was not what she had expected. And it certainly was not what I expected. I think what I meant to say was, "Anita, I sure hope you are staying here tonight because we have both had too much to drink for me to be driving to Calera." But I didn't say that, and now it was too late to change it. Anita immediately got up and looked for her coat. We were out the door in two minutes. I drove her home to Calera. There was little conversation. There was no goodnight kiss. There was no hug. And it was painfully obvious that there was no future for us.

My mother told me Anita asked about me from time to time during the next few weeks. More weeks went by and I just didn't call her. I always meant to. After a couple of months, it had been too long. I never talked to her again and my mother never mentioned her to me again.

Chapter Eight

In between my arrangements and dates, I would get bored and reply to someone on the website. I just had to be busy doing something and the something I was doing was having sex with a lot of women. And the site made it so easy.

During one break from the action, I received a message from an attractive woman who lived in Birmingham. She wanted to come out to my house immediately. She was about thirty minutes away. We agreed on terms, and she arrived a couple of hours later. This was faster than Amazon.

Rachel was about thirty years old and had a great body. I offered her a glass of wine. We drank one glass, and she was ready to go upstairs. She was uninhibited and knew exactly what she was doing. She even made me feel like I knew what I was doing.

When we had been in bed for an hour or so, it was all over, and she was ready to go. As she was getting out of bed she said, "You do know I'm a working girl, don't you?" I was so shocked by her candor that I thought she meant she had a day job.
Rachael did have a job. She was a "dancer" at a popular local strip club. She was getting a little old for this and had decided to diversify.

Around about this time I began to have some doubts about what I had gotten myself into. But right after sex is not a good time to make long-term commitments. They seldom last. In my case, it was all just beginning.

Chapter Nine

In Ghana, Africa, internet scamming is an industry. I am certain there are large concrete buildings filled with men, computers, an internet connection, and some pictures of beautiful women. Hardly a week goes by that I don't receive a message from Ghana. After a while, they are easy to recognize. There are 196 countries in the world. I can spot a message from Ghana in about five minutes. The profiles mention states like Alabama, Ohio, and Mississippi but these women are located in the western African country of Ghana, if they are women.

Felicia's profile said she was in Columbus, Ohio. When she finally told me she lived in Ghana, I asked her why she had told me she lived in Ohio. She told me her cousin lived there and she was staying there with her when she wrote her profile. This was total bullshit because it is virtually impossible to get out of Africa and come to the U.S. But she was beautiful. So, I pretended to believe her.

Felicia wanted to come to Alabama and marry me. No dating. No engagement. She just wanted to get married. We messaged for a couple of months. She sent me pictures. She even called me a few times on my cellphone. She was young, beautiful, and in love.

After about three months, Felicia began to ask me to help her get to the U.S. She told me she would need several documents including a health report, a police report, a passport, a visa, and an airline ticket. Of course, all of these things would cost money. I didn't know at the time just how difficult it was to get out of Africa. Scamming is so commonplace in Ghana that the airlines warn everyone not to purchase tickets from there. Most of them won't even sell tickets from Ghana if the purchaser is from another country.

Unbelievably, I began sending Felicia money for the documents. She always sent me copies of everything. They all looked very official. As I have said, it's an industry. In all, I sent about $1,000 to Ghana. It could have been much worse. When I began to try to purchase her airline ticket I ran into problems, but I am a very industrious person, and I was finally able to purchase Felicia a ticket on a Lufthansa flight from Accra, Ghana to Frankfort, Germany. The cost was about $2,200.

When all of this was done, Felicia told me her country required me to send her some spending money and funds for her return trip to Ghana. It seems that some American men have arranged for these women to come to America only to leave them stranded here. These were American men scamming African women! But this sounded reasonable to me. Did I mention she was beautiful?

Finally, however, I began to see this entire relationship was based on a very simple scam. When I told Felicia that I wasn't sending any more money to Africa she became very upset. I don't think it had anything to do with love. The truth is that I was a relatively rare fish they had hooked, and they weren't going to let me get off the hook without a good fight.

When I saw the African number on my cellphone, I assumed Felicia was calling. It wasn't Felicia. It was Felicia's agent. The agent told me I was breaking the heart of this young, innocent African girl and he was not at all happy about it. He said he wasn't playing any games with me. To make things right, I needed to give him my credit card information so he could set up a cash account for Felicia, and then everything would be just fine. He said he would personally put my "wife" on the plane. I hung up the phone. He tried to call me several times over the next few days.

As it turned out I was able to get a refund from Lufthansa for the airline ticket. So, I was out about $1,000 and a lot of time and effort. I was also embarrassed.

There is a little table at Walmart where you fill out forms to send money. There is a sign on that table that says, "STOP. DON'T SEND MONEY TO SOMEONE YOU HAVEN'T MET!" You wouldn't think a warning like that would be necessary. After all, who would do a damn fool thing like that? I think I mentioned she was very beautiful.

I receive a message from someone who says they are in Ghana every few days. I can usually recognize them immediately. My first question is, "Where are you located now?" There is usually some hesitation because virtually everyone knows Ghana's reputation. Then they might say something like, "I was born in Texas." Then I repeat the question. When they admit they are in Ghana, I immediately wish them all the best. Then I block them and delete their messages.

Chapter Ten

The Seeking Arrangement dating site was designed for just the kind of relationship I had with Susan. It was a great arrangement. It lasted off and on for more than a year.

Susan sent me a message that simply said, "Hey, sexy!" That got my attention because I can't imagine that it's true. I think it's called marketing. Susan was an attractive thirty-nine-year-old mother of a lovely nine-year-old daughter. She is a great mother. Yes, I understand some will say that's impossible, everything considered. I simply disagree. There were many times during our relationship when her daughter needed her, and we always changed our plans so she could be a mother. Her daughter came first. Everyone knows mothers who put their kids first. And everyone knows mothers who don't. I can introduce you to a few who don't, if you are interested in the experience.

We messaged on the site for a couple of days. For those of you keeping notes, two days of messaging is about average. After that, we began texting. After a few days of texting, we decided to meet at Seasons 52 for lunch to see if there might be a connection. However, one day before our date, I was on the site and noticed that her financial support was listed as "substantial." Most women don't pay much attention to this question and just check any box. That is a big mistake because "substantial" means more than $10,000 a month. That put her way out of my budget. I immediately texted her and apologized for not noticing her expectations and told her I didn't want to waste her time. She told me she liked me and wanted to meet me for lunch, and she had wanted to eat at Seasons 52 for a long time.

Parenthetically, here is a theory I have about women. Yes, I know how dangerous this can be—so, let's just call it an observation. I have observed that most women like to be pursued up to a point. That is just the way it works. After that, you need to back off a little, and in some cases, you need to retreat. As you are retreating don't be surprised if the woman is right behind you. Yes, they want to be pursued but they also don't want to be rejected. When Susan insisted that we keep our lunch date, I believe she saw my attempt to cancel our date as rejection. But I have been wrong about women a couple of times.

We had a very enjoyable lunch at Seasons 52. She asked me what my monthly budget was. I told her it was way less than what she was expecting. I gave her my monthly budget figure and she said, "What the hell, I really like you. Let's give it a shot." And just that quickly we were in an arrangement.

The next time we met, Susan came to my house for lunch. I made some sandwiches, and we drank a glass of wine. When we moved to the sofa, she almost immediately put her hand on my leg. That is one of my favorite things. But it was a little surprising to me. It had been some time since I had been with a woman who made the first move and it turned me on. We did it right there on the sofa. It never even crossed my mind to go upstairs.

Susan was very aroused and aggressive. I have been with some good actors, but when a woman is this wet, it's not acting. I had forgotten about the sex drive of a thirty-nine-year-old woman. Some experts think this is the peak for women. I was so surprised that I mentioned it to her. She said, "You will soon discover that I really love sex." And she was right. It didn't take long before we were in a very comfortable routine of meeting a time or two every week for sex. We also met occasionally for dinner or lunch. Yes, it was just an arrangement, but aren't all relationships arrangements? This one was looking like it might have long-term potential.

Susan asked me to build her a pine bed. So, we went to Home Depot and picked out the material. It was a labor of love because I knew we would be using that king-size bed from time to time in the future. The project turned out well. I put it together with some angle iron and black bolts. It had a rustic look. But it was sturdy and heavy. We had to disassemble it to get it into her house. One of Susan's friends even asked me to build her one. I declined.

As I predicted, she called me one day and asked me to come to see the bed after she had put it all together. It was beautiful. It was all white with big pillows everywhere. It was raining. She asked me if I would like to try out the bed. Well, hell yes. She cracked the door that opened out onto her deck. There is a lake behind her house. The rain was coming down now. You could hear it in the trees and on the lake. There was a gentle breeze nudging the curtains by the door. There may have been a better setting for sex but I wasn't present at the time. It was just perfect. She was thanking me for the bed, and I was thanking whatever gods may be I was alive.

We did get along well. She was fun to be around, and the sex was great. She was smart and didn't take any of my shit. She needed me but she could have done just fine without me. She told me many times that it was just an arrangement. She said she was not going to get serious about anyone for a long time. I believed her, right up to the day I ended the relationship.

From the very beginning of my online dating experience, I knew it was only temporary. I felt certain I wanted much more than an arrangement. And I knew I didn't want to spend the rest of my life alone. Eventually, I would find someone special. It might take a while, but I knew I would find my soulmate.

About that time, I met Alana on Mingle2. From the time we met, I thought we had long-term potential. I felt like she might be the one. Alana and I were hiking one day near my home, and she asked me if I was dating anyone. I told her I wasn't, but I had an arrangement. She asked me what that was. I told her. I don't lie. It's not a moral issue. It's just that my memory is terrible. I can't remember the lies I have told. But candor and truthfulness sometimes have unfortunate consequences.

When I told Alana about the arrangement she said in her "Asian" accent, "What the hell?" She asked me why I would ever do such a thing. I told her that a good friend once told me, "Buddy, let me give you some good advice. If it flies, floats, or fucks, rent it." I love jokes and I had always thought this one was really funny. Alana failed to see the humor. A good joke must have a scintilla of truth in it. I guess there was just a little too much truth in this one to be funny to her. In any event, she told me if we were going forward in a relationship, I would have to end my arrangement with Susan. Alana called Susan "the sweater girl" because she had left a gray J. Crew sweater in my closet when we first began our arrangement. Come to think of it, it's still in my closet.

I agreed to end the arrangement with Susan. I texted her and asked if she could meet me at Seasons 52 for lunch. I remember her saying, "It must be a special occasion." That should have given me a clue about the meeting. But it didn't.

I wasn't dreading the meeting with Susan too much. Our relationship wasn't going anywhere. The math wasn't right. I was too old for her. She had a young daughter. Most importantly, she had told me early on that she was not interested in a serious relationship.

So, when our wine came, I told her immediately that I had met someone. When I saw the look on her face my opinion about the meeting went south. Somehow, I had forgotten that little thing about a woman scorned. Hell, I thought it was an arrangement, and I told Susan this. She said, "What we have is much more than an arrangement to me. I like you." She didn't say she loved me.

I ordered more wine. Susan told me I was making a huge mistake. She told me Alana and I had not been together nearly long enough for her to be making demands on me. I think I mentioned Susan is very smart. As it turned out, she was also clairvoyant.

When Alana and I crashed and burned, I was tempted to call Susan and see how she was doing. But

I just couldn't bring myself to call her after the way I had ended the arrangement. I didn't have to call her, though; she called me. She told me she knew it wasn't going to work for Alana and me. Women are so damn smart.

I told Susan I was having second thoughts about arrangements. She said it was okay if we were just friends. So, we became friends. I think they call it friends with benefits. We started pretty close to where we left off—but not quite. I could tell there was some resentment there and I didn't blame her for that.

Susan and I are still friends. We have gone out and had some good times together. She called me one day and asked me to meet her at Oak Mountain State Park. She had taken some paddle board lessons and she wanted to show me her moves. So, I went down there, rented some equipment. We had a ball on the lake.

I haven't seen Susan since that day on the lake. It has been a few months. She has moved on with her life. I have moved on with mine. I would be surprised if I never hear from her again. People circle back when you least expect it. After all, we are friends.

Chapter Eleven

I have always had a weakness for beautiful Asian women. I know you are thinking I have a weakness for all women. You might be right. But Asian women are special to me. I have so much respect for the Asian work ethic and their traditions. And many of the women are strikingly beautiful.

I met Alana on a dating site called Mingle2. She was a beautiful fifty-six-year-old woman. As I have stated, one of my internet dating rules is that I don't make the first move. My profile and recent pictures are out there so I simply wait. In the case of Alana, I thought she had real long-term potential. So, I broke my rule.

Alana and I chatted for a couple of days on the site. She didn't seem at all interested but she did agree to a phone call. The first thing I told her was about my weakness for Asian women. I thought it was a great pickup line. It was perfect. But her reply was, "I am not Asian. I am Pacific Islander." Then it got worse.
I said, "Well, you certainly look Asian."
She replied, "Well, I'm not Asian."

Now, I'm not saying that all Asian people look alike to me. But that is exactly what she thought I was saying. I had never even heard of a Pacific Islander. I certainly have now. I have heard it about a million times.

Somehow, we got past my social blunders. As we talked on the phone for the next few days, I tried to think of something I could ask her to do with me. I was trying to think of something that would be hard for her to turn down. She had mentioned that she occasionally liked to just get in her car and drive around. So, I finally asked her if she would like to go on a one-day road trip to Mentone, Alabama. Mentone is in the mountains of north Alabama. There is a nice park there with a beautiful waterfall. Randy Owen, the lead singer of the group Alabama, lives nearby. It is a very romantic place.

When I picked up Alana at her house, I noticed several cars in the driveway. There were two Mercedes and a new Toyota Highlander. I thought something might have happened. It certainly looked like she had company. But she was home alone. All of the cars belonged to her.

So, this woman had a big house on an estate lot and drove several expensive cars. This was unchartered waters. This woman was different. This woman was not desperate.

When Alana invited me inside her home, I was immediately surprised at what I saw. The house was decorated very formally. I am a big Frank Lloyd Wright fan. All of this French furniture was a little too much for me. But I wasn't there to give her interior decorating advice. I was there to start a relationship. I am much more qualified in that area. Notice, I said *start* a relationship.

It was early June, but a huge Christmas tree was still standing in the living room. There were also many other elaborate Christmas decorations throughout the house. It reminded me of one of those Santa Clause parks where it's Christmas year-round. I can barely stand it for a few days.

Tucked in among all of the Christmas paraphernalia was a shrine to her late husband who had died three years earlier. His ashes were there along with some other religious items. I discovered over the next several days that Alana was still very much in love with her deceased husband. She talked about him often and his picture was still on the screensaver of her cellphone.
The road trip to Mentone was fun and relaxing. I know it sounds corny, but it seemed like we were meant to be together.

Alana had told me early on that she was not ready for a physical relationship. I knew it had everything to do with her late husband and I also knew it could take a long time to change that. It crossed my mind that it might never change. One day we were sitting on my front porch swing drinking some wine. Yes, that magic wine. I asked her how long she thought it might be before she would consider intimacy. By intimacy I meant things like touching, hugging, and kissing. I knew sex was out of the question.

A technique I have used often in business dealings and my relationships is the shock factor. I will sometimes ask a question that is unrelated to the topic of conversation. You would be surprised how candid some of the responses are if the other person doesn't have time to fully consider her answer. I think that's what happened with Alana. Because her answer wasn't some convoluted bullshit. Her answer was, "It will take thirty days."

I asked, "Thirty days?" Then I asked her, "Why exactly thirty days?" She couldn't answer that question. So, I asked her, "Why not thirty hours or thirty minutes?" I am such a shit sometimes. Why did I have the full-court press going? Needless to say, she was not impressed with my argumentative style or my NCAA basketball defense.

A few days later things began to change. Since we had been together, I had exercised inordinate caution when it came to anything physical. You might think it was because I am a gentleman. It wasn't that at all. I thought if I touched her, I would never see her again. I remember us sitting on my front porch when she unexpectedly put her naked leg in my lap. I was shocked. I saw this as an unusual and aggressive move, and I decided to counter with an even more aggressive move. I put my hand on her leg. She didn't resist. Her inhibitions were almost gone but she was not ready for sex.

I don't know the reason, but I decided to use the Bill Clinton definition of sex in my approach. I told her we could wait on the sex, but I would be happy to make her feel really good. She told me that oral sex was her weakness. I about fainted. I will leave the details to your imagination. It wasn't long before we had left the Bill Clinton definition and were having the real thing. Yes, I know I am leaving out the fun part here, but I am just trying to be nice.

Alana was a very noisy lover. I am certain that some of my neighbors will remember those initial sexual episodes. I asked her occasionally to try to be a little quieter and she said she would try. Then she would scream and moan so loud when she climaxed that I worried that someone would call the police to investigate.

Despite all of this passion, there was very little affection. There was no hand holding. There were no kisses. At least there were no kisses on the mouth. There wasn't even a goodnight kiss. I thought this was extraordinary and I told her. Again, she asked me to give her some time. I gave it my best effort. But I just couldn't relate to making the trip from passionate sex to hand holding. It was the exact opposite of what most people consider normal. It was like saying, "You guys need to be careful; all that fucking could lead to some serious touching."

After a few weeks, Alana did come around. She became very affectionate and intimate. She would tell me, "I told you it would take thirty days." And, as it turned out, it had taken almost exactly thirty days.
Our relationship began to seem normal. It was hard to believe how far we had come. We were together several times a week. I began to give her some financial advice and we occasionally talked about how convenient it would be if we lived closer together. I even took her to visit my mother in Calera. Asian people have so much respect for the elderly. And my mother and I both fit that description. And, yes, I know Alana isn't Asian but that is what I called her. She thought it was funny. Mother and Alana liked each other, and mother was finally happy with my love life.

When we had been together for about two months, Alana became somewhat suspicious and jealous. She wanted to know exactly what I was doing and who I was doing it with. She also wanted to know everything that was on my cellphone. Well, like people's cellphones, there is a lot of confidential information on mine. Alana would tell me a dozen times or more a day, "Let me see your phone." She would try to look when I entered my passcode, and she would try to maneuver my thumb over the home button on my iPhone. In early July 2015, a dear friend asked me to go with him to Lima, Peru, where he was going for embryonic stem cell injections. James has a condition called idiopathic pulmonary fibrosis. IPF is a terrible disease because the low oxygen levels and the stiff scar tissue in the lungs make it very difficult to breathe. James was already carrying oxygen with him everywhere. He was in pretty bad shape. I did some research on the internet and didn't see where embryonic stem cell injections had been at all effective in treating his disease. When I told him this he said, "Okay, the doctors here have given up on me. This is my last hope to stay alive. So, what are you suggesting?" That's when I bought my ticket to Peru.

After a few days, I began to think about what I would do for a week in Lima, Peru. James would be at the clinic for hours every day, and I would be alone in the hotel room or walking around the city. So, I asked Alana if she would like to go to Peru with us. I was surprised when she said yes. I bought her a ticket, and we began planning the trip.

We had a great time in Peru. We ate ceviche and drank pisco sours every day. James got his injections during the day, but he was free in the evenings. Being there with James was the right thing to do. As I am writing this, two years later, I am happy to report that James is doing much better. Most of the people in his support group are either worse or dead. Virtually all of his symptoms are gone. His doctors now are saying he will likely die *with* IPF rather than *from* it. They call it a miracle. But the only difference between his treatment and the treatment of the other patients is the embryonic stem cell injections. This procedure is not allowed in the United States. I think it has more to do with religion than anything medical. Maybe if the word embryonic was eliminated it could be approved. What a shame.

Right here is as good a place as any to tell you about an incident that happened in Peru that changed my relationship with Alana forever. Months before the Peru trip, I had been chatting with a woman from, of all places, Ghana. I think her name is Mary Aju. Out of the blue, there was a message on my cellphone from Mary. I shot her a quick reply that I was in Peru. She said she wished she could be there with me. I said something like I wish you could too. I was just trying to be cordial and get her off my phone. At that moment, Alana grabbed by phone and the figurative shit hit the proverbial fan.

Look, I know I should have ignored that message from Mary. I was trying to be polite but that is no excuse. I was wrong. But the damage was done. Beginning at that moment, Alana's suspicions went into warp mode. Her questions were constant and suffocating.

Soon after we returned home from Peru the questions and accusations reached a peak. At the time, I was going through a difficult period with my mother's healthcare and with my estranged brother. The pressure that Alana was bringing to the table was becoming almost unbearable.

Alana was at my house late one afternoon. She was about to leave to go home. She said, "I will see you tomorrow."

I don't know exactly what was going through my mind at that moment, but her words pulled a trigger in my brain; I said, "Alana, could you give me a couple of days to focus on some family issues?" You would have thought I had called in the Napalm.

She said, "What the hell do you mean?" In a very few seconds, this sweet little, easy-going "Asian" woman was down on the floor begging me not to leave her. When I tried to move away, she grabbed my ankles and held on tight. I don't remember the lies I told her to get her out the door. I do know it took a long time and I know I would have said anything to get it done. Alana had just gone completely berserk over a simple request for a little breathing room. But this is all from my perspective. I am certain her view was completely different.

During the next few days, it only got worse. Alana showed up unannounced at my door several times. She came to my house when I wasn't there and waited for hours until I returned. I was keeping a young grandson at the time, and his parents were becoming concerned. I told Alana if she didn't stop her nonsense, I would call the police and let them handle it. I blocked her on my phone. Those two things helped, but she then began calling my friends and family. I have to admit it was a little scary for a few days. Most people thought she was capable of about anything during this time. I knew she was just trying to deal with a broken heart.

A few weeks after this unexpected and incredible breakup, Alana sent me a very passionate and heartbreaking email. It was only after reading this email that

I began to understand the intensity of her pain and suffering.

Here is her unaltered email:

August 10, 2015

My Love,

I want you to know that since the day we met I've fallen in love with you. There are no words to express the feeling in my heart the day you came into my life, and how you make every day so special. I have waited for so long to find the right person, and then I found you in such an unexpected place. I have loved you since the day I told you to clean up your act and you did all the things that I have asked you to do, and what did I do? I ruined it because of my fear to fall deeply in love again. I was scared to love you at first, out of fear that you would hurt me, but I did, and it's been the best thing I've ever done. Now, the only fear I have is waking up and realizing it's all a dream.

Loving you is the only thing that makes my life worth living. Day by day, my love for you becomes overwhelming, and I can't handle it when I don't see or even talk to you every day. I love you more today than I did yesterday, and I will love you more tomorrow than I do today.

I apologize straight from my heart for pushing you further and further away from me. I realized that you did all you can do to be near to me. I am sorry for all the heartache that I have caused you.

A day without you in my life is like a day without sunshine. I need you when I am cold to keep me warm. I need you in the rain to keep me dry. I need you in my life to keep me happy. You make me feel wonderful. You give me strength when I just can't carry on and I truly treasure that. Every moment we spend together is another one of my dreams come true.

I'm afraid I'll say something to make you forget the feelings you have for me when I mentioned your past too much and bring up stupid and hurtful words. I'm worried you won't want me anymore. I know I can make you mad, but I promise you that this is all going to change because I love you with everything I have. Please give me a chance to show you that I have changed, and that you are my priority, and I will love you until the end of my days.

You are the most wonderful thing that has ever happened to me. Each moment that you and I spend together is so magical that I catch myself smiling for no reason at all.

Honey, you completed me. You make my life so amazing, and I don't know how else to repay you but to love you just as much as you love me. My world is a better place to be because of you.

Thank you for giving me so much more than I ever could have wanted. I am so thankful for what we have. You are the only man I ever want to share my life with. I could never imagine what it would be like if I were to lose you forever. I don't even want to think about it. All I want to think of is you.

If we never get back together, just know everything I have said is true, and always will be true. I love you from the bottom of my heart. My love for you will never fade. I'm still crazy (not literally) about you.
Love you always,
Alana

    It has been a long time since I received that email. Alana called me almost every day for several months. She has been dating someone for over a year now. A guy she met online. She told me she is committed to him. She tells him she loves him. She calls me a friend. I asked Alana many times to stop calling me. I told her I didn't need any more friends. I even asked her how her lover would feel if he knew she was calling me every day. But she kept calling me. I honestly don't know why. Sure, I could have blocked her calls. I could have told her to just leave me alone. Occasionally, I determined that I would do all of that. Then I would go back and read her email and it broke my heart. Again. Eventually, the calls ended. I guess her broken heart finally gave up.

Chapter Twelve

I don't know why so many Black women reach out to me on the internet. I usually ask them that question. They give me answers, but I don't think I will ever completely understand it. A third of the women I am writing about are Black. More than half of all the messages I receive are from Black women.

Jessica is a beautiful 29-year-old Black woman from just south of Chattanooga, Tennessee. For reasons that will soon be obvious, I can't show you a photo of Jessica. I wish I could, because you would be shocked at her beauty. You might be a little shocked anyway.

I realize that some of you who are reading this will think that all of these women can't be beautiful. You say there simply aren't that many beautiful women out there. Well, this isn't Walmart. There are two other reasons why you are wrong. First, ugly women don't do well on Seeking Arrangement. Second, I only chose to meet about 10% of the women who contacted me. I almost always choose the pretty ones.

Jessica told me she wanted to drive to Birmingham and meet me. I told her it was a two-and-a-half-hour drive and that she shouldn't be going to the homes of strangers. She told me she was an excellent judge of character and that she loved to drive. I am not good at arguing with beautiful women. I guess my heart just isn't in it.

It may have become obvious by now that there is much more I could say about the sexual component of these various relationships. I have condensed hours of sex down to a few minutes of text. My theory is that the imagination is a pretty good storyteller. But the story about Jessica simply can't be told without including the graphic sexual component because Jessica is a squirter.

I had heard of these women off and on for years, but I had never known one. I mean known as in the biblical sense. I had no idea what it would be like. Yes, I know the definition of the word squirt, but that is not enough information to be very helpful. In any event, I certainly wasn't prepared for Jessica.

Most of the women I have met are not nearly as modest as I had thought they would be. When I ask if they want me to turn the lights down, for example, they usually ask, "Why?" So, I usually just leave the lights up. This has the added benefit of helping me with my objective of paying closer attention to everything this time around. This does add a new dimension to sex.

Jessica has a nearly perfect body. Her breasts are firm and are just the right size for me. Just a little over a handful. I helped her get those little puppies out in the open where they could breathe better. Just in case, I gave each of them a little mouth to mouth. Well, you know what I mean. We took our time with everything. I don't think it could have been much better.

During the extended foreplay I asked Jessica how she felt about using a vibrator. She said she had never tried one, but she had always wanted to. I thought I had a small unit in the chest beside my bed, but for some reason, it wasn't there. So, I went into my bathroom and grabbed my Sonicare electric toothbrush from its stand. This isn't as kinky as it might sound.

First, it's a great little vibrator, and second, if your mouth is going to be there anyway, what difference does it make? That's my story and I'm sticking to it.
We were still taking our time. She was hotter than a two-dollar pistol. She was very wet, and she was making those female sounds that I just love to hear. I know where to look for the G spot and I had found hers.

When I touched her with the toothbrush she came almost immediately. Even if she had warned me that she squirted I would not have been prepared for what happened. It was in my face, in my hair, on my chest, and the bed. Just to think I could cause a young woman to do this was one of the most erotic things I could ever imagine.

Jessica never said a word about her squirting. I guess she thought all women did this and it was normal. But every time we had sex after that first time, I had several towels ready. The towels didn't seem to bother her one little bit.

Jessica made several trips back to Birmingham to see me. She invited me to her place several times. I never visited her. I don't know if she liked me, or my toothbrush. I didn't care. I still think about her occasionally. I might be a little old fashioned, but I think someone you are intimate with becomes a part of you forever.

I have been told a lot of women fake their orgasms. I can tell you that Jessica wasn't faking hers.

Chapter Thirteen

Her pictures were nice, and her profile was interesting. Jessie said she was a cosmetologist who lived and worked in Adamsville, Alabama. She was a thin and beautiful 27-year-old woman with long blond hair. The first time she contacted me on the website, she wanted to come to my house that very day. I told her I could not meet her that day. I didn't expect to ever hear from her again. Several weeks later she messaged me again and asked what I was doing. I told her I was working out. She asked if she could meet me later in the afternoon.

Most of the women I have met online want to meet for lunch, dinner, a cup of coffee, or a drink at some public place. I have recommended that policy to virtually every woman I have met. They don't ask for my advice and seldom take it, but I give it to them anyway. It's difficult not to give fatherly advice to women of this age. This is particularly true for young women who are doing something as inherently dangerous as internet dating.

Jessie didn't seem to care about meeting me in a public place. So, I lost another argument with a beautiful woman. My record isn't impressive.

Some would argue that any woman you meet on a dating site like Seeking Arrangement is a prostitute. I have had several friends tell me this. Indeed, most people feel this way. I completely understand this position. The only problem is that it simply isn't true. I am not saying there aren't prostitutes on the sites. There certainly are. But not every woman on these sites is a prostitute. Some women won't ask for financial support. Some women will indeed ask for rent money or money for their car payments. A few will just quote a flat monthly allowance figure. Virtually all will negotiate. I readily admit we are in a gray area here. I don't think there are fifty shades, but the dominant color is gray.

I would estimate that about 20 percent of the women on the Seeking Arrangement site are prostitutes. Only about half of the twenty percent admit it. That is their problem, not mine. Jessie would not consider herself a prostitute. She asked me for $500 every time she came to my house. I think that makes it pretty clear.

I had told Jessie that $300 was at the very top of my budget. She responded, "That is fine sweetheart; because once you have been with me you will pay me whatever I ask in the future." I like a woman with confidence. Some might call this kind of talk marketing. I call it bullshit.

When Jessie arrived, I was very impressed. I was thinking she might be right about what she was worth. I was pleased with my negotiation skills. She was exactly as advertised. She was very attractive, and she was nice. We sat down at my eating bar and I asked her if she wanted a glass of wine. She said yes. I don't think she ever touched her glass. We talked about our experiences on the site for about thirty minutes. I told her about a young woman from Memphis who had stolen my new iPad. She looked genuinely shocked.

The simplest and most common scam a prostitute must guard against is not getting paid. They all handle that by simply insisting on getting the money upfront. I completely understand that. She mentioned the money and I reached in my pocket, took three one-hundred-dollar bills out, and put them on the bar. That seemed to help her relax.

After Jessie had been at my house for about forty-five minutes, she told me she had a headache. I asked her if she wanted me to get her some ibuprofen. She told me ibuprofen didn't work very well for her and asked if I had anything stronger. I told her I would give her half of a Percocet if she liked. She said that would be great.

I went upstairs to my bathroom medicine cabinet to get the Percocet. I was gone less than a minute. I'm still amazed at how quickly and quietly Jessie got out the front door with my $300. She is quite an athlete, and I was quite a fool. There might be a simpler scam out there, but this is about as fundamental as it gets. It's so simple that no one would think it could happen. I certainly didn't think it could happen, but I was thinking with the wrong head at the time.

Now, I had Jessie's pictures, her cellphone number, and other personal information. It would have been relatively easy to hire someone to find her. A lot of men in my position would have done just that. Yes, I know it would have cost me a lot more than $300, but that misses the point. A lot of men would have been seriously pissed. Jessie had put herself in this position for a measly $300. Now, that is desperation.

I did send Jessie a text that I was going to find her no matter what it took. Then I simply forgot her. I had learned a very valuable lesson and it had cost me only $300. That's a real bargain.

Unbelievably, Jessie looked at my profile again within the following couple of weeks—the site informs you when that happens. I didn't even send her a threatening message. Maybe it was because I just wanted to forget about how foolish I had been—no maybe about it; that was the reason.

Chapter Fourteen

I usually reply to messages from everyone who reaches out to me online. I think it's just rude not to at least say hello. But I'm just not interested in fat chicks. Sorry, that's just the way it is. Of course, you won't find the word fat in the profiles. These fat women describe themselves as "curvy" or as carrying "a few extra pounds." Some who say they are "average" are fat. Occasionally, you will see BBW in the profile. I had to google this to find out it meant big, beautiful women. The term "pleasingly plump" is also used. A popular online dictionary says this about that term: "A term commonly used by desperate fat women looking to get laid. These plus-size women like to run personal ads describing themselves as 'pleasingly plump.' Sure, you're pleasingly plump if the arctic is refreshingly cool." I could not agree more. I understand this is small and judgmental. I don't care.

Ashley did have such a pretty face. She described her body as average. And you couldn't tell by her pictures that she was overweight. She was very young. She was street legal, but barely. I told her she was way too young for me, but she kept contacting me, and I finally agreed to meet her for lunch at a little Italian restaurant in Alabaster, Alabama. She was very sweet, and she wanted to try out this internet dating thing. She also had champagne taste that she was trying to fund on her beer budget. That is where I was supposed to come in. She was so damn cute and sweet that I agreed to give it a try.

I want to make it clear that Ashley was not obese. At about 35 pounds overweight she is likely average in America. But average in America is fat. Other than her few extra pounds, her body was flawless. She was also clueless. She desperately wanted to make it happen but just didn't know how. Her biggest problem was that she had a difficult time doing what she said she would do. And that doesn't work for me.

Ashley began sending me nude pictures. She sent me selfies of everything. I don't know how she got herself into some of those positions. She begged me to see her again. She told me she would do better. She promised everything. I liked her, but I just wasn't interested. Incredibly, Ashley continued to text me for over a year. She told me she loved our time together and she can't find anyone she enjoys being with as much as me. I told her it was nice hearing from her, but my life is just too complicated to get back into a relationship with her. I don't tell her it's because she is fat. After all, I am such a nice guy.

Chapter Fifteen

Sandra said she lived in Lexington, Kentucky. She saw my picture and profile on Mingle2 and messaged me. She immediately sent me some beautiful pictures of herself. They were selfies, but she had done a great job with the composition. I don't understand why some people are so photogenic and some of us aren't. She was an attractive 28-year-old woman with short brown hair. She said she was bored and just wanted to get out of town for a few days.

Sandra asked if I would mind if she hung out with me for a couple of days. She told me she might drive on down to the beach after that, but she wasn't sure. I told her she was welcome at my house as long as she wanted to stay. We even discussed going to the beach together.

She was a smart woman. Her texts were well written, and she said all of the right things. Then she said, "Could you send me $70 for gas to get to your house?" I had gotten pretty good at judging people by then. Yes, I had made some obviously dumb mistakes, but I had learned from those mistakes. Yes, I had decided I would never send money to someone I hadn't met. But Sandra was so nice and so convincing I decided to break my rule. It was only seventy fucking dollars.

I am not going to tell the story of every one of my relationships. Some of them are too similar and that would get boring. I am not mentioning Sandra because I pissed away $70. That isn't important. The important thing about Sandra is the way she handled the scam. So, listen carefully.

Asking for gas money is the most common scam on dating sites. It is so simple. Anyone can do it. A man with a computer and pictures can do it easily. I am certain this happens often.

When I sent the money to Sandra, the scam was done. She had my money, and I would never hear from her again. At least that's what any reasonable person would think. What happened was a different story.
Sandra thanked me for sending the gas money. She told me she couldn't wait to see me in Birmingham. She told me her departure had been delayed for an hour because her mother wanted her to stop by her house for a few minutes. An hour later, she texted me and told me she was on her way.

A couple of hours later, she told me exactly where she was on the interstate. She said traffic was unusually heavy, but she would make up the time when she got on I-59 past Chattanooga, Tennessee.

Then she texted me and told me there was highway construction going on in Chattanooga, and she might be thirty minutes late. Twenty minutes later she texted me again and told me she was hungry and had decided to stop and get something to eat.
I never heard from her again.

She had my money. Why did she play with me for hours? I will never know for sure but here is my guess. Most women have been hurt by men. Most of them just move on with their lives and try to make better decisions. But a small number of these women have decided that all men are bad, and they are hell-bent and determined to get even. What Sandra did for several hours had nothing to do with me or the money. It had to do with getting even with some man who had done her wrong. Bless her little heart.

Chapter Sixteen

When I saw her username, I should have known she was a stripper. Angela had the most beautiful little caramel body I have ever seen. She was about five feet four inches tall. She had a small waist, and her breasts were just over a handful and were perfectly shaped. I couldn't resist taking pictures of her and she loved the attention.

She and I met on the Seeking Arrangement website, but I don't think she was looking for an arrangement. I'm not saying she wouldn't consider a sugar daddy, but she loved what she was doing, and she was perfectly suited for it. She and I were together many times. We never had one disagreement. She knew what she wanted, and she knew what I wanted.

The first time I saw Angela, I met her at a shopping center, and she got into my car. She was driving a new red Lexus convertible sports car. Sex is big business and those who do it well make a lot of money. She did it well.

The moment Angela got into my car I could smell the weed. I asked her if she smoked in her new car. She just smiled and said, "All the time, honey." She would buy those little cigars with the wooden tips, remove the tobacco and fill the shell with marijuana. The result was a very neat way to smoke pot.

I wouldn't allow Angela to smoke in my house. That odor lingers for a long time, and I didn't want everyone to think I was doing the shit. So, she would go out on the back deck and smell up the entire neighborhood. I have no idea how she functioned, smoking all of the time. I had smoked weed a time or two in my life and it didn't do much for me.

On one of Angela's visits, she asked me if I wanted to try some. I was a little uptight for some reason, and I didn't see what it could hurt, so I took two small hits. When we came back into the house, I hardly knew where I was. I was talking with her, and I completely lost my train of thought. I told her I had forgotten what we were talking about. She smiled again and said, "It's the weed, honey." And it was. It was by far the strongest I had ever had. Again, I don't know how people can do this and walk around. I guess the human body can adapt to just about anything.

Angela and I didn't have a regular thing. Occasionally she would call me and ask what I was doing, and she would come over. She has asked me many times to come to the club and watch her dance. She told me she would treat me like a king. I have never gone. The last time I was in a strip club was a long time ago, and the memory of all the cigarette smoke is everlasting.

The sex with Angela is good. I know she likes me because she could be with just about anybody. That makes it good. If there isn't some sort of chemistry or connection, it's just not worth the time and effort—not to mention the money.

Angela is a nice woman. Yes, I know that sounds strange, but she would never hurt anyone purposefully. She does what she says she will do, and she never has anything bad to say about anyone. The sex isn't terrific with Angela because she isn't a kisser. And sex cannot be great if there is no kissing.

Angela's body was just about perfect

Chapter Seventeen

Lisa works at Home Depot. I met her on Seeking Arrangement. She was working full time and going to school at night. She was living with her mother, but she wanted to move out so she could have some privacy. Moving out required more money than she had. She was desperate.

Lisa is a very attractive Black woman in her early thirties. If you see her in Home Depot, you will recognize her immediately because of her looks and her great personality. She has a beautiful smile, and she flashes it often.

We messaged for a couple of days on the site, but we were soon texting. She wanted to meet me, and we decided on breakfast at Cracker Barrel in Calera, Alabama. We were supposed to meet at 9:00 a.m. I arrived at 8:50 a.m. and waited. At 9:30, Lisa had not arrived. She didn't call or text, she simply didn't show. This happens occasionally and is almost always a deal-breaker for me. I think that's a good rule to have and I recommend applying it religiously—except I'm not religious.

I decided to text Lisa and ask her what happened. I thought there was a chance I might have been mistaken about the time or the place. When she replied to my text, she apologized and explained she was at the emergency room with her mother who was very sick. I thought this qualified as a valid excuse but how much time does it take to send a text? I had driven an hour and that could have been avoided. I spent my entire career in the construction business. It was my observation that a project that began in trouble usually stayed in trouble. I can say the same thing about relationships.

A few days later I received a text from Lisa. She asked me to give her one more chance. Her mother was now home from the hospital, and she had some free time because she was in between school terms. She had not met anyone she was the least bit interested in on the website, and she liked my pictures and profile. As they say, flattery will get you everywhere, so I agreed to meet her for coffee.

Lisa is a smart lady. She is a survivor, and she will always land on her feet. She isn't afraid of work, and she is very ambitious. Her only issue is that she has a little chip on her shoulder. I don't understand the reason for this. She seems very confident but there is just a tinge of paranoia in her personality. It's like she is expecting people to treat her badly. I assume it has something to do with her past, but you know what they say about assumptions.

Lisa and I decided we would have a probationary arrangement. We would just see each other occasionally and see where it went. She came to my house and where it went was to the bedroom.

There is something about making love to a strong-willed woman that turns me on. Of course, my switch is usually in the on position, but this is different. One moment the woman is acting like she rules the world and is immune to anything and the next moment she is on her back moaning and placing my hands on all of her favorite spots. Lisa had a lot of favorite spots.
I know it is a control thing. It's the same reason some beautiful women are attracted to men in positions of

power. For example, this recently happened between the governor of Alabama and a staff member. She is attractive. He is not handsome. But he was in a position of power. I say *was* because the governor was forced to resign over the alleged affair. Speaking of power, there is nothing more powerful than sex. I realize I am not breaking any new ground here.

Lisa and I saw each other occasionally for months. We only had sex a few times, but I liked her. I still occasionally get a text from her that says, "Hi, stranger." We exchange a few texts and then I don't hear from her for months. I haven't seen her in a long time, but she is on my mind every once in a while. As I have said, when you are intimate with someone that person becomes a part of you forever. It can be a very good feeling. It can also be a very bad feeling.

Chapter Eighteen

There aren't many men who don't dream of having two women in the same bed at the same time. I doubt there are many men who have lived this fantasy. It isn't that easy to find this opportunity, but there are offers out there from time to time. At the time, I had two important items on my bucket list. One project was to get a tattoo, and the other was to arrange a threesome. First, I got a tattoo on my upper arm, and then I began looking for a threesome. I wasn't looking that hard, but I did have my eyes open for the opportunity.

I have always said I would consider a threesome, but the other two people in the bed would have to be women. I am not the least bit judgmental when it comes to gay people. I know they are hardwired that way and I don't have a problem with it. Some of my friends think you can "pray the gay" out of someone. I think that is bullshit.

But not being judgmental and being in the same bed with another man are two completely different matters. I just don't think I could get and sustain an erection if I knew there was another penis that nearby. And I think that would be highly likely.

When I read the profile that said, "two for the price of one," I couldn't resist. The women were in their early twenties, and both were lovely. They weren't quite beautiful, but they were quite attractive. I had seen several profiles that mentioned a threesome option, but they usually involved an attractive woman who had a not-so-attractive friend.

Now, I know you are thinking that I have finally crossed the line into pure prostitution. And you would be correct in that observation except for one thing — these women have real jobs and are just trying to earn some extra money by dabbling in the world's oldest profession. And I think what they do with their own body is their business. I have never been called liberal, but I think mine is a somewhat liberal position on that subject.

There is no reason to go into great detail about this event. Well, except that it is erotic and a little kinky. We didn't meet for coffee or lunch. We didn't text for days. We agreed on a price and the two young women appeared at my door. They were exactly as advertised. They looked exactly like their pictures, and they came in the door smiling.

We did take the time to have a glass of wine and talk for a while. They were very interesting women, and they loved to talk. I could tell they were more than friends and that was fine with me. After about an hour, I began imagining them naked in my bed upstairs. I think they could read my mind — or my body — because one of them asked if we were going to get in bed together. I liked the way she was thinking.

The women were not the least bit inhibited. They began to take off their clothes as soon as we got into the bedroom. It was obvious they had been in the same bed together before. I left the light on because I didn't want to miss anything. Their bodies were young and restless. This was going to be everything I had imagined.

Three people making all of the love sounds at the same time is a very erotic and incredible experience. It was one of the most exciting things I have ever done. I would do it all over again, but one time is likely enough for me.

This is going to sound strange but here goes. While the ménage a trois experience is incredible, it is a little confusing at the same time. I think if you did this regularly you could sort it all out. But if you are used to being in bed with one person, and then you are in bed with two people at the same time, it is difficult to change sexual gears. I found myself having to think about what I was doing. That detracted from the experience. But somehow, I managed.

We were in bed for about an hour. They were in no hurry. One of the women had an orgasm or two and the other didn't. I think the one who wasn't orgasmic was a little upset that her lover was having so much fun. But it could have been something else.

The bed was a mess. Covers were on the floor, the sheets were wrinkled and wet, and the smell of sex was pervasive. It was perfect.

The young women didn't stay around long afterward. That was fine with me because I was exhausted and wanted to go to sleep. I don't know why I was so exhausted. Well, maybe I do know.

Chapter Nineteen

I trade houses like some people trade cars. And I trade cars even more often, so I spend a lot of time at the county license office. When I walk in, one of the clerks will usually ask me, "What have you bought now?" They know me well and I usually chat with them if there is no line. One of the clerks works the information desk in the front and she isn't busy all of the time.

I had just purchased a 911 Porsche in Atlanta, and I was at the license office to register the car and pay the sales taxes. As I was leaving, Debra told me she had heard I was divorced. I told her I was. Then she asked if I was interested in dating a friend of hers. I told her I might be. But I was thinking that was highly unlikely. I certainly wasn't buying a pig in a poke. Yes, I know that sounds like a Freudian slip. Hell, maybe it is. It simply means buying without inspecting the item beforehand.

Debra's friend had asked her if she ever saw anyone come into the license office whom she might be interested in dating. Debra had told her I was the only one who came to mind. That was a surprise to me, but it made me feel good at the same time. She gave me her friend's name and number and told me I should give her a call. I waited a couple of days to call. I didn't want to appear desperate. I was desperate, but I didn't want anyone to know.

When I first saw her name on the little piece of paper, I thought it sounded familiar. I thought it was likely a coincidence. It wasn't a coincidence. I didn't know the woman, but I knew her ex-brother-in-law, and I knew some of her other relatives and friends. Her ex-husband's family owned a large construction company in the area, and they were well known throughout the state. This woman might be desperate, but her desperation almost certainly had nothing to do with money.

Margaret was a very attractive woman in her mid-fifties. After I called her, we exchanged photos by text. She was older than most of the women I had dated and that was a good thing. This woman was a southern lady, right down to that familiar southern drawl.

At about this time in my internet dating program, I was beginning to think I would never find anyone who would even be a candidate for a long-term relationship. I can see that smile on your face and hear you humming that old song, "Looking for Love in All the Wrong Places." I think I hear it too.

All of this made me excited about the potential this relationship could have. After all, she had reached out to me.

After Margaret and I texted for a couple of days, we began trying to arrange to meet for the first time. I was flexible but it was just before Christmas, and she had a hectic schedule. Her sister was in town and the family was busy with the holidays. She finally invited me over to her house for dinner. I stopped by Whole Foods on the way and picked up some food from their kitchen and a bottle of good wine.

Margaret lived alone in a large house. She would later put the house on the market for $1.4 million. She moved first, and then put her house on the market. Not many people can do that.

When she came to the door, I immediately thought this could work. I was determined not to run her off by appearing too anxious. I would have to be at my very best.

I opened the wine and poured two big glasses. We ate dinner and chatted. She talked inordinately about her ex-husband, their divorce, and the continuing financial issues. Almost every topic was about her family or her church. I knew the question was coming and I was prepared for it. But there is just no good way to tell an evangelical Christian that you are having serious doubts about the very existence of their one and only God. There are some good reasons not to discuss religion but, in some cases, it just cannot be avoided.

My theory is that atheists and Christians are very close to believing the same thing. Christians have eliminated every single god in the history of the world, except for one God, out of the thousands of choices. Atheists have simply added one more god to that list. But I digress.

Margaret was shocked at my lack of faith, and I completely understood. You don't meet that many people in this part of the country who don't profess to be religious. Certainly, most people aren't as religious as they claim to be, but they will never tell anyone. It's much easier just to go with the flow.

Despite her initial shock, Margaret seemed to dismiss the issue quickly. She suggested we move our conversation into her den. She sat down in a large comfortable-looking chair. I sat down near her on one of the sofas. She said, "Why don't you come over here and sit with me?" It never crossed my mind to sit in the chair with her, but I did as I was told.

She immediately told me she would never consider a relationship with anyone until she determined if he was a good kisser. I had seen and heard about everything by this time in my recent dating life, but these two moves were unexpected. I am not a shy person. I was using extreme constraint because I thought one false move could end the relationship before it began. I didn't know exactly what to do.

Out of an abundance of caution, I asked her if she would like to begin the kissing evaluation now. She said, "Why do you think I brought up the subject?" That was about as clear an invitation as I have ever had, and I accepted it. The kiss turned into a smooch and that turned into a little good old-fashioned foreplay. Then it was over. She announced that I had passed the test with flying colors. I hadn't won the game, but I felt like I had hit a home run.

I wanted to stay with her, but I knew better than to mention the subject. I could have been wrong. I will likely never know. I elected to end the evening on a perfect note. The perfect note had been sung and I knew it couldn't get much better that night.

I told her I knew she was busy with her family and with Christmas. I asked her if I could call her and she said, "Of course." I kissed her goodnight and left.

I didn't call Margaret for a few days. When I texted her, she seemed busy. A few more days went by. I finally texted her and asked if she had changed her mind about us. She told me she had a relationship issue she was trying to resolve, and she could only promise me friendship at this time. So, there was another man she was trying to decide what to do with, and she wanted to keep me in a holding pattern until she made that decision. I told her to call me when she got her issue resolved.

I likely made a mistake by saying that to her. If I had accepted the friendship role I would have been there when she made her decision. That's the good news. The bad news is I would have been there when she made her decision. I didn't think I could take that risk.

Almost a year later, Margaret called me from the Mayo clinic. She was undergoing tests for a brain problem. She had been falling a lot lately and she had finally hurt herself. We talked for an hour. I remember telling her she might want to consider wearing a football helmet everywhere. She thought that was funny.

The purpose of her call was to invite me to a party at her new house. The party was a fundraiser for a local kid's charity. A national celebrity was coming to entertain. She also told me she had acquired a wine cellar full of old wine that she knew nothing about. She wanted me to come over and help her sort it out. She was thinking of selling some of the more valuable bottles. I told her I would be happy to come over any time. We set a date and time a few days from then. A day before we were supposed to meet, she texted me and told me she had to go to the doctor, and we would have to delay our meeting. She never rescheduled.

I couldn't attend her party either. By this time, I was going to Ukraine regularly. I would be in Kyiv on the night of the party.

I haven't talked with Margaret since that phone call canceling our meeting. I began to think her rather bizarre behavior regarding our relationship could have been caused by her brain issues. I guess that's like saying she would have to be crazy not to like me.

Chapter Twenty

The vast majority of contacts never result in meetings, much less actual relationships. A woman might favorite you on a site. Then, she will begin messaging you. After a while, you are texting and exchanging pictures. A potential relationship could end at any time in this process. Sometimes, I simply don't reply. Other times, I stop replying when I think the woman is from Ghana or is beginning a scam. You might think this is unusual. It happens very often.

Tracy, from somewhere in Indiana, asked for my cellphone number so she could send me a text. She immediately sent me a picture of a beautiful Asian-looking young woman. She began asking all of the usual questions like what I was looking for in a woman. I told her, "I'm looking for love. Ideally, it would be long-term love. I'm looking for just about anything but bullshit."

She asked what I was doing for the rest of the day. I told her I was writing a book. She said she was looking for "someone to always be there for [her] and a man of his word. [She was] tired of cheaters and game players." I told her this texting meant nothing to me. There must be a meeting, or we are wasting time. She said, "The ball is in your court. You make the call and I will follow. I am looking for a long-term relationship. I want something to hold on to and give my life a new meaning." At least she knew the English language.

I told her she was welcome to come to Birmingham but, "I can't send money to someone I haven't met. I hope you understand."

She replied, "Yes, I completely understand." Of course, they all say this. Otherwise, the conversation is over, and the object is to keep it going. A salesman once told me if he could get a customer to say no three times, he knew he would usually close the sale. That is the theory of women like Tracy. And it worked.

Tracy began asking about the book I was writing. She seemed to be genuinely interested in my new baby. I sent her the draft of a chapter. She read it and said she liked it. She said she wanted to read the whole book. She asked for another chapter, and I sent it to her. I was interested in her feedback because she appeared to be intelligent and well read.

We continued to text for a few days. Tracy sent me some more pictures of herself. When I asked her if she wanted to come to Birmingham she replied, "If I get the invitation, then I will honor it."

I said, "Tell me how you would get here since I don't send money to someone I don't know."

Her response was, "Can you do me a favor?"

Let the record show that I knew the scam was on at this point. But this was a scam with which I was unfamiliar. I just had to find out what her next move would be. It didn't take long.

Tracy said, "I have a check I need to cash. Can you do that for me, please? At least I will have enough money for my trip to you and a little shopping before I come."

I said, "Sure, I will cash it for you if it's a certified check and I verify the funds are being held."

I thought this would end the conversation, but she replied, "Sure, it is a certified check."

"Tracy, why would you ask me to cash a check that any bank would cash for you where you are located?" She immediately replied, "Because there is no way I can cash any check at any bank other than my bank and I have closed my account there, so there is no way I can get the check paid." I asked her how she intended to get the check to me.

Tracy said, "I just received an email from my former employer, and they want to pay what they owe me. The accountant has decided to make the payment by check. The problem is I no longer have a checking account. I was hoping you could cash the check for me. I will have the accountant mail the check directly to you. I am owed $1,950, but I think there will be the usual deductions. The company will be issuing the check and it will be made out to you."

Of course, none of this was making any sense. I certainly should have stopped texting Tracy and blocked her at, or before, this time, but I was intrigued. I just had to see what her next move would be, so I played along. I told her, "Okay; if my bank clears the check, I will cash it for you."

I gave her an address for mailing the check and we resumed talking about my book. It was easy to talk about because I was writing between texts with her. She asked how many words I had written, and I told her about 45,000. She told me she was looking forward to being around someone who was a writer and a reader. This woman had bullshit down to a science.

The next day Tracy sent me a text that read, "I really hope we meet soon. I just got word from the accountant, and you should have the check by Tuesday. That means I can be with you before Thursday. I plan to take the train or a flight. Which one do you think is best?" I said it would depend on where she is located. She said, "I am in Oregon."

Yes, she first told me she was in Indiana. Now she was in Oregon. She told me she was in Oregon for an interview, but she lived in Indiana. I said, "I think that's bullshit."

She said, "I am not lying to you, baby. I meant everything I have ever said to you, and nothing is going to stop me from coming to you. Do you believe me, baby?"
I replied, "No."

She continued her passionate texts for the next couple of days. It was her usual talk about being together and having fun. I replied to her texts occasionally. It's difficult to be nice when you know you are dealing with a crook.

Tracy was tracking the check and she soon told me it was in Birmingham. She was texting me often now. She wanted to know if I had been to my mailbox. She wanted to know if I was going to take the check to the bank immediately. She was getting a little anxious.

When I saw the check, I was surprised. It was written on a local Alabama bank from a real estate business in Mobile. I immediately googled the real estate company and it appeared to be a legitimate business. I decided to call the business and verify the check. When I asked if they had written me a check they asked, "Why would we do that?" The check was for $1,750.09, and it was an official company check.

The lady asked me to email her a copy of the check. I did this, but the company email firewall would not accept the attachment. Five minutes later, the owner of the business called me. I sent him a picture of the check on his cellphone. He confirmed it was a real company check. He thanked me for being honest and told me he was turning the check over to the fraud prevention department of Regions Bank and they would be in touch with me.

The next morning, I received a phone call from the lady at the real estate business. She told me three fraudulent company checks totaling over $6,000 were cashed the previous day. She thanked me again for not cashing mine.

There is no way of knowing how big this scam was. It might have been nationwide, and it could have very well been connected to organized crime. But I likely will never know. One thing is for certain, it was a felony and a federal offense because of the FDIC and the USPS. These weren't petty thieves. And it had all started with a pretty picture on an internet dating site. I never heard from Regions Bank. They reimbursed the real estate company, and the bank was likely covered by fraud insurance. The people who will pay for this crime are all of us banking customers. We will pay with increased fees and interest charges.

The man who owned the real estate company had asked me to play along with her until the bank could investigate the matter. I told him I would wait until noon the next day. By then, Tracy had texted me several times asking about the money. At 12:30 I texted her, "My bank has turned the check over to the FBI."

Tracy had my address and cellphone number. I wanted to scare her into leaving me alone. I immediately blocked her on my cellphone. In a few minutes, I received a call from an "unknown" number. I get those occasionally, so I wasn't concerned. Then the phone immediately rang again. This time, "No Caller ID" appeared on the screen. Then it quickly rang two more times, and I knew it was connected to the scam.
Five minutes later, my cellphone rang again. This time the message on the screen read, "+234 806 403 9937 Nigeria."

I knew if I answered that call there would be a man talking to me in broken English. He would be warning me to send him the woman's money or there would be hell to pay. A little voice deep inside was telling me to leave it alone. A louder voice was the unmistakable voice of my father saying, "Son, you traded for it."

Chapter Twenty-One

Connie lived in Memphis, which is well outside my normal hunting radius. But she was young and beautiful, so I decided to reply to her message on the site. She immediately sent me her cellphone number, and we were off and running.

Connie had all the right stuff. I could go into detail about all of her stuff, but she isn't included in this story because of what she had that belonged to her. She is here because of what she has that is mine. Connie is a thief.

She insisted on coming to my house in Birmingham. I asked how she planned to get here. She asked me to send her money for a bus ticket. By now, I know better, and I offer to purchase her a bus ticket online. This offer usually ends the conversation, but it didn't with Connie. She told me she wanted to spend a couple of days with me in Birmingham on her way to Atlanta.

The Greyhound bus website has a map on it that lets you see where a bus is located at all times. I'm sure they use the same GPS that is used by trucking companies to keep up with their fleets. The map is a very cute trick.

When Connie's bus arrived in downtown Birmingham, I was there to pick her up. We drove directly to my house. We put her bags in the bedroom and went out to get something to eat. She was very hungry. We spent the rest of the day tooling around the neighborhood on the golf cart. I took her fishing at the lake on the property. Her father had taught her to fish, and she caught several large bream and one small bass. She had a good time.

The next couple of days were fun. We went out to eat once and we picked up food and brought it to the house. We also spent a lot of time in bed. We were sitting on the front porch swing late one afternoon when she took me by the hand and led me straight upstairs to the bedroom. I loved this. I can't recall it happening to me before.

But, as I suggested, Connie isn't in this story because of all the wonderful sex. She is in this story because when I took her to the bus station, she had my new iPad and some other items in her bag with her. She was smooth. It never crossed my mind that she might be a thief.

Early on, I had a problem with women stealing drugs out of my medicine cabinet. I should have anticipated this, but I didn't. Percocet and Valium are valuable commodities. They are easy to sell, and the price is high. After I installed a combination lock, I had no other problems.

It took me a couple of days to notice the iPad was missing. I knew immediately where it was. It was in Atlanta with Connie. Unfortunately, a few days later my credit card statement came in the mail, and I saw where she had stolen my credit card information and used it to make purchases in Atlanta. She had bought some food at Chick-fil-A and, more significantly, she had purchased a round-trip ticket on American Airlines to Miami, Florida.

Of course, I immediately canceled the card. Visa investigated the matter and refunded everything to my account. So, I was only out the iPad, but it pissed me off. I texted her and gave her a piece of my mind. Surprisingly, she replied to my text. She apologized for everything and promised to send me the money when she received her federal income tax refund. The IRS has been incredibly slow with that refund.

Since the experience with Connie, I keep a closer eye on my wallet, and it is never alone in the same room with anyone. It takes about 15 seconds to take a picture of both sides of a credit card with a cellphone camera and that is all you need. You can use the card for online purchases with no identification. It is so easy. It is too easy.

Chapter Twenty-Two

Shelbyville, Tennessee, is about a three-hour drive from Birmingham. When I received a message from a young woman from there it barely got my attention. But she wanted to text. I gave her my cellphone number. She texted me immediately and asked if she could come to Birmingham and meet me. I asked her if she knew how far it was and she said she did.

Donna was not beautiful. Like most of the others, she was young and desperate. I told her it was too far, and I wasn't interested in seeing someone from so far away. I told her it didn't make any sense. I should have been telling myself that because I was right. It made no sense. That should have been a red flag. But by this time, I had ignored so many warnings, what was one more?

I told Donna there must be a modicum of chemistry or it just isn't worth the time and effort. I said all of the negative things I usually say when I am not sure. I even told her I would only pay for her gas if nothing happened between us. She insisted on coming anyway. What else can you do?

The answer to that question is you can tell her not to come. And that is exactly what I should have done. Someone once asked Carl Sagan what his gut feeling was on a particular subject. His response was, "I try not to think with my gut." I agree, but my gut was telling me something was wrong. I wasn't listening. I didn't care if Donna came or not. I just wasn't thinking clearly at that time. That was a big mistake.

By now, I knew what I was doing could have unexpected consequences. I had simply let my guard down and I was about to suffer the consequences.

What happened next was not complicated. It didn't even bother me very much when it happened. But it was one of the most dangerous things that happened during my two years of internet dating.

When the bell rang, I went to the door to find a rather small and childish woman standing there. She looked scared and hungry. Her eyes were wide open, and she was very nervous. I didn't see a vehicle out front, so I asked her where her car was. She told me a friend had brought her and he was waiting for her to call him to pick her up. I asked her to come in and sit down. Then I asked her what her friend was going to do for a few hours. She told me not to worry about him. He had gone to get something to eat and he would be fine until she called him.

We talked for about thirty minutes. She was still very nervous. She should have been nervous. She should not have ever put herself in that position. But she wasn't nervous for the reasons I would have warned her about.

I poured Donna a half glass of wine. She didn't touch the glass. I told her I was not comfortable with the situation. When she had been there ten minutes, I knew nothing was going to happen. I wasn't interested in anything with her. I just wanted her to leave. When I told her this, she asked me about the money I had promised her. I reminded her I had offered to pay her gas money. She wanted $300. I asked, "For what?" She said for the time she had spent with me. I gave her $40 for gas. She called her friend.

About three minutes later, there was this loud banging on the front door. Donna got up and I followed her to the door. When I opened the door, there stood a young man about 6'6" tall and weighing about 300 pounds. I could immediately tell his elevator didn't go all the way to the top of this tall building. He told me to give his friend the money. I told him I had given her exactly what I had promised. He told me she had promised him $100 for driving her to Birmingham. I pulled a twenty out of my billfold and gave it to him. He then demanded the $300.

The window of opportunity to avoid this crisis had long since passed. I had no choice but to open the door and let Donna out. Now I was facing a brute who was demanding money.

I have a gun-carrying permit. I have a Taurus Judge revolver that shoots .45 caliber cartridges and .410-gauge shotgun shells. I keep it in the chest by my bed. I also have a Smith and Wesson .38 caliber revolver that I usually keep in the glove compartment of my car. Tonight, it was in the pocket of my jeans. The gun was loaded with defense rounds. That load makes a small entrance wound and a huge exit hole. I have two rules regarding self-defense: don't pull a gun unless you are prepared to use it, and don't use your gun unless you are prepared to kill someone.

Instead of reaching for my gun, I pulled my cellphone out of another pocket. Brutus asked, "What are you doing?"

I told him, "I'm calling the police to come to sort this out."

He said, "You are a crazy old man."

I told him, "We are about to find out who is crazy in this group."

At this point, anything could have happened. He could have killed me with something he had brought with him. Hell, he could have killed me with his bare hands. If he had made one step inside my house, I would have shot him dead. Instead, he turned and ran down the front doorsteps. Donna was right behind him. They jumped into a car and sped off.

When they had been gone for a few minutes, I received a call from Donna's phone. It was Brutus. He said, "Old man you got lucky tonight. I could have squashed your head like a watermelon." And he could have. Or I could have shot him and been in for a real messy house cleaning job. Either way, it would have been a very bad day. The stage was set for a tragic ending. All the actors were in place. One tiny move changed everything. When Brutus turned and ran down the steps, it might have saved someone's life. And that is incredible.

Chapter Twenty-Three

I have overused the term beautiful. Not that the ladies aren't beautiful. But after a while, it just begins to sound like they are all drop-dead gorgeous women. That isn't the case.

However, Linda is beautiful in every way.

When I saw her pictures on Seeking Arrangement, I remember thinking she was as beautiful as any of the women in the fantasy pictures my friends emailed me about once a week.

I sold my Harley Vrod last year. On one of my last rides with friends, we ate breakfast at IHOP. Bikers aren't picky eaters. When they asked what I had been doing since my divorce, I showed them some pictures. They were flabbergasted. They didn't believe me. After the shock subsided, one of my biker friends told me something unbelievable. He told me there was no way he could ever get in bed with a beautiful young woman. I asked him why not. He said he would be too embarrassed.

Think about that. These men send pictures of naked women to their friends. They do it often. But when it comes right down to it, most of them wouldn't think of actually having sex with one. There is this wide chasm between fantasy and reality.

I want to make it clear that I am not recommending my lifestyle to any of my married friends. I don't date married women. Hell, I'm not recommending my lifestyle to anyone.

In addition to her extraordinary beauty, Linda has a great sense of humor. Her profile was incredible. One thing she said was, "I can kick your ass at golf and drink you under the table." The golf part was bullshit. The drinking part wasn't.

Linda's pictures on the website were all glamour shots. You could tell they were done by a professional. So, when she came to visit me for the first time I was expecting just about anything. What I saw when I opened the door was incredible. It reminded me of the women in Ukraine. These women will cancel a meeting if they haven't had time to get ready. And "get ready" in Ukraine is not the same as "get ready" in America. The body parts that weren't already perfect on Linda were artfully made perfect by plastic surgery. The result was Venus.

Linda isn't recommended for the novice. She is a professional. She knows exactly what she is doing, and she will eat your lunch if you aren't careful. I once tried to entice her to my house using Dom Perignon champagne. She told me, "I can buy my own Dom." Well, excuse me.

I love a spunky woman. We have never disagreed. There was no drama. We just have great conversations and great sex. I take pictures of her, and she is happy to pose. She weighs in at about 110 pounds, but she will throw your ass on the bed and rock your world. She also just happens to give the best damn blowjob on the planet.

Linda came over to my house recently. It was wonderful. She asked me what I was reading. I told her I had just finished *Hillbilly Elegy*. She wanted to borrow the book. I agreed because I knew she would have to bring it back.

Chapter Twenty-Four

Emma messaged me on Seeking Arrangement. I use this dating service because more of the people are really there. There are also a lot of women there who live in the Birmingham area.

Emma lives in Bibb County, which is about forty miles southwest of where I live. We messaged on the site for a couple of days. I gave her my cellphone number and she texted me. She was in a relationship, but she wasn't getting nearly as much sex as she liked. She also told me she was a squirter.

It was a warning. She said she understood how squirting could turn some men off, so she just wanted me to know upfront. While it was something relatively new to me, it certainly didn't turn me off.

We decided to meet at the Bright Star restaurant in Bessemer, Alabama. It's a great place to eat and it was about halfway between us. When I arrived at the restaurant, the owner told me a lovely lady was waiting for me in a private booth in the back. That was encouraging.

Emma is a big, tall woman. She was once much larger, but she had lost about a hundred pounds. She was quite attractive. We had the usual great Bright Star meal and talked. After we finished lunch, Emma told me she thought she wanted to have an arrangement with me, but she wouldn't know for sure until we kissed. So, we kissed right there at the table. She told me I was a great kisser. We agreed on the details of the arrangement, and we were in business.

Emma came to my house a few days later. We chatted for a while. She was interested in the community where I live. We rode my golf cart around the neighborhood. When we got back to my house, she immediately wanted to have sex. And, I could see she had not been getting enough attention. I also saw why she warned me about her squirting. I had had one other similar experience, but I wasn't prepared for Emma. I still don't completely understand the phenomenon. I simply can't get over the quantity involved. It should not be called squirting. When I think of squirting, I think of the small water pistols I played with as a child. Based on my limited experience, sexual squirting should be called gushing.

I was surprised at the quantity, but I was also surprised at the frequency of the orgasms. After sex, I was lying there with my hand on her and she squirted again. I thought I had seen just about everything. Now, I know that is impossible.

As I mentioned, Emma had lost a lot of weight. There was a lot of loose skin everywhere. When her clothes were on, it wasn't noticeable. When she was naked, it was unavoidable.

Emma was in her early forties and very sexual, but I had been spoiled by some young perfect bodies and I just couldn't go back. We met one more time and the arrangement ended. It was entirely my fault. She called me and wanted to come see me, but I knew it was just a matter of time before I would not be able to perform under those conditions. And it's supposed to be fun.

Chapter Twenty-Five

I was getting increasingly harder to please. I was also beginning to realize that this merry-go-round had to stop eventually. I wasn't ready to settle down, but I knew it wouldn't be long before my focus would turn to a long-term relationship. About this time I met Amy.

I had stopped by a little Italian restaurant a few miles from my house to pick up some food to take home. I was waiting to place my order when this attractive woman walked in the door. She was alone. She looked around like she might be meeting someone here. She walked toward me. She had a beautiful smile. She spoke to me. She was waiting to be seated.

I asked her if she ate here often. She told me she was a regular. I asked her if she could recommend something good. She told me the lasagna was very good. I asked her if that was what she was having. She said no she was going to eat a salad.

I have always wondered why I haven't met women in the usual places. I have worked out at a gym for forty years. I have seen some lovely women there and a few have smiled at me. But I have never actually hooked up with a single woman at the gym. The same is true for the grocery store. I hear of it happening all the time, but it has never happened to me.

At least part of the reason it hasn't happened to me is that I am a little shy. I hear you laughing. Stop. Also, I am a little nervous about invading someone's private space. I need to be invited in, and that is simply not the customary male role. These past two years have given me a new perspective. Yes, I am less shy, but I am also aware that beneath the don't-give-a-shit façade of most women, there is a desire to connect. And it is the man who usually makes the first move. But there is also the possibility of rejection. Hell, it's complicated.

I made the first move with Amy. It was so easy. I asked, "Are you eating that salad here, or are you taking it with you?"
She said, "I'm eating it here."
Then I said, "I'll share my lasagna if you'll share your salad." She said okay.

I was so proud of myself. I'd made a connection the old-fashioned way. This was so damned cool.
We sat down at a table and waited for our food. Joe's Italian is a great little restaurant in a little strip center not far from my house. Yes, I know how that sounds, but it's true. Trust me, I've eaten in thirty countries, and I know good food.

Amy was in her mid-thirties. And while I had a long-term relationship in mind, what can you do when a beautiful woman interrupts your plan? I was in transition. You might I say was tapering off.
This reminds me of the joke about the woman who caught her husband in bed with a midget. She said to him, "You told me you would never be unfaithful to me again!" He replied, "I'm tapering off."

Soon after we began our conversation, I had the feeling we had met. It wasn't a pickup line. I just had this feeling. She told me her father had developed a lot of property in the immediate area and she told me who he was. I immediately made the connection. I knew her father, who was about my age, and I was an investor in one of her brother's businesses!

All I could think about for the rest of the meal was what is Jason going to do when he discovers I'm dating his sister? I know I was thinking way too far down the road but that's just the way I think. Jason was going to kill me, and we were going to have to reconsider our business dealings. Shit.

Before we left the restaurant, we exchanged contact information. She gave me a little hug and I headed for home. This traditional dating scene was really weird.

A few days after our meeting at the restaurant, I texted Amy to see if she might be interested in seeing me again. I could tell she was a busy young lady because she was always driving somewhere. She had a daughter about six years old and that also kept her busy.

Amy was thirty-six years old when I met her in 2016. I considered her too young for a long-term relationship with me, but I was headed in the right direction at least. She agreed to meet me for lunch and after a while we were seeing each other a couple of times a week.

Of course, we eventually worked our way to the bedroom. She has a nice body. Her ass is nice and round and her breasts are big and firm. Yes, a little large for me but I am learning to deal with this issue. I'm so adaptable.

After a couple of months with Amy, I wasn't that interested in seeing anyone else. Occasionally an old friend would circle back around, but I wasn't actively searching for another woman. It was nice just settling down and not worrying about what I was going to do on the weekend. I knew I would see Amy every few days and that was enough for me.

I introduced Amy to some of my friends and we went out together from time to time. We sometimes went to Chuck's Fish for seafood or Seasons 52 for some wine and flatbread. We had a normal relationship—except for the age difference and her six-year-old daughter. I liked Amy and she liked me. I believe she wanted to keep it going but I knew it was not long term. And a long-term relationship was what I was looking for.

About two or three months before I met Amy, I had decided that the United States of America was not large enough for my search. So, I expanded my happy hunting-grounds to Eastern Europe. I had seen the pictures of beautiful Russian women, and I just couldn't resist taking a closer look. I don't have any idea why I neglected the entire balance of the Western Hemisphere but that's exactly what I did.

Chapter Twenty-Six

I did some research on the internet and settled on a Russian dating site called Ukraine Brides. Yes, I know Ukraine is no longer a part of Russia. But most people in those previously Russian countries speak Russian as their first language and many still consider themselves Russian.

As the name implies, Ukraine Brides is about finding husbands for women on the site. It is what my family later referred to as "a mail- order bride shopping center." They were trying to be funny, but I liked the concept.

During the last few weeks of my relationship with Amy, I was communicating with some women on the Ukraine Brides website. Amy and I were not committed to each other. We both knew there were likely too many issues to overcome. But we were certainly having a good time together. Whatever happened, I knew we would always be close.

The next chapter in my life was a yearlong whirlwind romance that began on the other side of the planet and ended in Mexico. The issues are many. The ups and downs are a rollercoaster ride. So, buckle your seatbelt and secure any loose items. I didn't fasten my seatbelt and some items flew out that I will never be able to replace.

Part Two

*"Come on baby, don't say maybe
I gotta know if your sweet love
is gonna to save me."*

"Take it Easy" by The Eagles

Introduction

Does anyone ever know the moment they fall in love with someone? I doubt it. But when Oksana jumped into my arms at the Opera Hotel in Kyiv, Ukraine, I certainly felt like this was the real thing. She told me she fell in love with me months later. I am not certain she ever did.

Chapter Twenty-Seven

It was in October of 2015, when I finally decided to contact some women on the Ukraine Brides website. I had heard of all the Russian dating scams, and I had no idea whether this site was legitimate. When I saw all of the beautiful women there, I seriously questioned how this could be real.

I used the same strategy on Ukraine Brides I had used on Seeking Arrangement. I posted my profile and pictures on the site and waited. The response was immediate. I received messages from several gorgeous women in just a few hours.

These dating sites make their money a lot of different ways. The first way is messaging. The lady can send you a message for free but if you reply, you must pay. You purchase credits online using a credit card or PayPal. Each time you send a message, the site debits your account. The site shares the revenue with the ladies. No wonder the messages came fast and furious.

Initially, it was difficult to ignore a message from a beautiful lady who wanted to meet and marry you. It just seemed rude. After you spend a few hundred dollars in just a few days, it gets a lot easier.

Another way the sites make money is by delivering gifts. You can purchase almost anything—from flowers to food—on the sites. The sites debit your account and deliver the gifts to the ladies.

You can't message a lady directly. You must use site messaging. The site reads every message. If there is any kind of personal contact information in the message, the site will refuse to send it and issue a warning. If you want contact information you must purchase it from, you guessed it, the site. The contact information typically costs about $250 each, and the lady must agree to provide the information. Most dating sites advertise free membership, but the membership is virtually useless unless you are willing to pay a lot of money for the services.

Ukraine Brides did everything they promised. When a gift was delivered, they sent me a picture of the lady receiving the gift. When they arranged meetings, the ladies were always there. The initial meeting with a lady cost $100 for the first hour. That cost includes a very qualified translator. After the first hour, you pay the translator about $10 an hour for additional help. These charges might not seem like a lot of money, but they add up quickly. Also, you pay about double the price for everything. For example, a bouquet that costs $100 on the site can be purchased in Kyiv for less than $40. You pay a lot for the service, but the service is good.

It is difficult to determine whose messages to answer. They are almost always well written. I am sure the site helps with the message content and with the translation. The more replies these messages generate, the more money the site and the women make. And, of course, it's all your money.

I might have replied to a dozen different women on the site. After a while, I narrowed my communications down to just a few and eventually to three of four. Within a month, I became interested in only one woman. Her name is Oksana. Oksana is a very common name in Ukraine. There are a lot of them on the site.

Asking Ukraine Brides for the archived messages was an afterthought. I thought it might help me more accurately recall the timeline of my story. As it turned out, the messages became an essential resource for confirming chronological events and emotions. It changed the story. Ironically, it made the story less believable but more accurate.

For example, I had no idea how unreasonable I had been in my dealings with Oksana. I didn't remember being so controlling. I don't know why she didn't tell me to get lost on many occasions. Who could blame her? Also, there is no way I could have ever accurately remembered the events between January and June of 2016. As I read the messages, I still couldn't believe we held our relationship together for that long considering the distance and the incredible issues between us. I don't think my story could be complete without including some of the actual dialogs between Oksana and me. Of course, there is no way to include all of it. It is hard to imagine a stack of over a thousand letters and thousands of Viber messages. So, I just picked out a few of the letters to convey the feel of the moment, and to try to help you and me understand how this all could have possibly happened.

Chapter Twenty-Eight

Our messaging relationship seemed to blossom quickly. Oksana was very interested in me and wanted to talk often. After all, she was getting paid by the message. I don't have any idea how much money I spent messaging Oksana on the site. It might have been $1,500. It could have been much more because we communicated virtually daily on the site for eight months before we met. I tried to purchase her contact information many times, but she always refused. I think this was the first red flag I noticed in our eighteen-month relationship. It would not be the last.

Ukraine Brides archives online messaging on their site. As I was writing this chapter, I decided to ask them for a copy of my messages with Oksana. There were 1,007 messages from November 2015 through July 2016. We began messaging in October, but I assume messages are deleted after some period. Eight months is a long time to send messages without meeting. I can't believe I did it. I had never been anywhere near this patient about anything in my entire life. And there is not a chance I will ever do it again.

In just a couple of weeks, Oksana and I were talking about serious issues. On November 3, 2015, I sent her the following message:

Dear Oksana,
I am sending you a couple of pictures of my house. I love my house, but there is something missing. YOU aren't in the

pictures! Do you want to be? I am so tired of the women I am meeting online. I want to find my soulmate.
I am retired and I have a lot of time for traveling and fun things. But I don't want to do these things alone. I want someone like you to do them with me.

I will be happy to do a video chat session with you. I am available almost any time. Just let me know. I will always be honest with you. You can ask me anything. I hope we can meet one day soon because that is the only way we can decide if we are right for each other. I hope you agree.
Sincerely

The next day Oksana replied,

Sweetheart,
Ever since I first saw you online there has not been a day that you have not been in my thoughts. Love has mysterious ways of working and I hope our love will blossom and grow. My dear, can you be honest and candid with me? I really need an opinion from a sociable and active man like you. For sure, relationships should be full of passion and hot things. But should it begin with sex? What might be the end of such a relationship?
What do you think? What is your opinion? Maybe you have had such an experience. Please share your opinion with me. KISSES! I am always waiting for you here or in chat. It is such a pity that my old PC doesn't have a working camera, but we can talk any time dear.
I am waiting!

So, the messages weren't simply, "Hi, What's up?" They were lengthy letters about very intimate subjects.

We talked about our physical and emotional needs and Oksana almost always asked me to send more messages or to join her in chat. Since I was paying by the message, I tried to limit my replies to about one message a day. Since she was getting paid by my replies, she usually sent four or five enticing letters a day.

On November 6, 2015, Oksana sent me a message on the site. She said, "Your lady Oksy is online now, and she is waiting on you for a chat date. Where are you? Do you not want to talk to me? You know, Joe, it is not good when your lady is waiting for so long. Are you not a gentleman? I want to kiss you at this moment. May I? Oksana."

Yes, she called me Joe. I replied, "I am not Joe." I asked her, "How many men are you talking to at one time, Oksana? Is it difficult to keep all of us straight?" She then went into a long explanation about her favorite singer, Joe Cocker. She said he had been on her mind. She told me her English wasn't that good and she often made mistakes. Of course, she also told me I was the only man she was communicating with on the site. Then she wanted to move on as if nothing had happened. But this was a huge red flag that I somehow ignored.

Chapter Twenty-Nine

During the next couple of weeks, our messages were the usual dialog between a man and a woman who were falling in love. We somehow got over the "Joe" hump and moved on. Then on November 25, 2015, Oksana sent me a message about the upcoming Thanksgiving holiday. She wrote,

My Dear,
You have a big holiday coming! How will you spend this holiday? Thanksgiving is not celebrated in Ukraine but I know how important the celebration is for you. I hope you appreciate my desire to be a part of it and to celebrate it for the first time in my life. I have read a lot of information on the internet and I decided to buy a turkey and cook it in my flat. A whole turkey will be too much for me so I will buy some part of it. Is this allowed?!!!
But, I don't know how to cook a turkey. Can I just roast it in the oven like I do with chicken? Or is there some special recipe I should follow? What can I do here to make my atmosphere like yours? How about the Macy's Thanksgiving Day Parade? Do you always watch it?
I miss you every day.
Oksana
PS: I had a dream of you and me last night, honey. Mmmmmmm.

I thought Oksana might be exaggerating about her desire to share the American Thanksgiving holiday with me. But I replied with some suggestions for roasting the turkey and I told her about some other traditions.

Then, on November 26, Oksana sent me one of the most beautiful and touching letters that she would ever write. She said,

My Love,
I am here with my dinner and a candle. I am celebrating my first Thanksgiving Day. I want to thank you, my dear, because you are the reason I am here now with warm feelings and grateful thoughts. There are not very many good people on the planet. So to meet you makes me feel especially thankful. Did you think we would ever feel the way we do about each other?
I hope you are surrounded by good people on this Thanksgiving Day. I wish you good health and success in everything you do,
My sweet kisses and hugs darling.
Oksana
PS: When you are sitting at the table, just know I am close by.

Sitting here these many months later, I can't hold back the tears when I read her words. How could the translation be so perfect? How could she choose the perfect words? Was it love or just some special gift she possessed? It really doesn't matter. The pain is the same.

It would be remiss if I didn't mention the possibility that the Ukraine Brides website could have written this perfect letter. It is certainly in their area of expertise and best interest.

I also want to mention the inordinate tendency of Eastern Europeans to celebrate. For example, Russians celebrate Name Day in addition to their birthday celebrations.

So, all Oksanas are honored with gifts and entertainment one day each year. It is a serious social blunder if this day is ignored. It's unthinkable.

Chapter Thirty

When Ukraine Brides sent me the archived messages it was in a spreadsheet format. I eventually downloaded the document in Microsoft Excel, but it was so long horizontally, and the font was so small that I couldn't read the messages. I mentioned this problem to a young friend who was over for dinner one evening. He asked if he could take a look. I opened the document and showed it to him. He made about a dozen clicks and the document was in paragraph form, the date of each message was in a column, the person sending the message was in another column and I could easily pick the font size I wanted. I felt pretty dumb.

When I saw the size of the reformatted document, I was shocked. If it had been printed in the same font as this book, with the same margins, it would have been over 300 pages. It took me a few days, but I read every message. It was one of the most emotionally difficult things I have ever done.

As I read the conversations through the end of November and into the first part of December, I saw something very different from what I remembered. Oksana and I talked almost every day about meeting soon. We were aiming for the middle of January. She said she had told her boss she wanted to be off around that time and he had agreed. I told her I was checking on the airline tickets and trying to decide on a hotel in Kyiv.

When all of this was happening, I was just trying to see if it was even practical to go to Ukraine with all of the political problems there. When I read the messages, it was clear that I was telling Oksana I was making plans to come. She was very excited to think that a man was going to do what he said he was going to do. A man was finally going to stop talking and be a real man for a change.

On December 14, I sent Oksana this letter:

My Dear Oksana,
I am so sorry to tell you I have some bad news. Today, December 14, the US Department of State issued a Ukraine travel warning. They are prohibiting travel to some cities in Ukraine and are advising against travel to anywhere in the country.
I called a friend in the government, and he told me the conflict between Russia and Ukraine factions had escalated in the past few days and I should seriously consider delaying my travel plans. He reminded me of the Malaysia Airlines plane that was shot down. That flight originated in Amsterdam and that is exactly where my KLM Airlines flight will originate.
I am so damned depressed about this. If you could meet me somewhere in Western Europe, I will pay all of your travel costs. I want to see you soon. I don't want to wait.
I am so sorry, sweetheart. I would do almost anything to see you but I'm afraid that doesn't include putting my life on the line. I am thinking about you while you are reading this letter. I wish I could be there holding you.
All of my love.

At the time, I thought this was a perfectly reasonable decision. When I read the archived message, it just sounded like I was indecisive and afraid. The response from Oksana was predictable.

Sweetheart,

How could you?! OMG! I even took my vacation from my job! I will not get paid for these days!

There are many foreigners in my country. They aren't afraid of Putin. Why are you afraid? The war is in the eastern side of the country. Kyiv is perfectly safe.

The war zone in Ukraine is where I live. Yes, there are bombs and I often see soldiers here. That is the reason I agreed to take a nine-hour train ride to Kyiv to meet you. I knew you were afraid from the beginning. How could you do this? Why didn't you tell me from the beginning?

I am crying! Some happy new year!

Lonely Oksy.

PS: And I believed you were the one real man for me!

    I wrote Oksana a very sincere letter of apology, but the damage was done. Looking back, I couldn't blame her for the way she felt. At the time, I thought she was being a little naïve about the war in Ukraine. Now I see that I should have been a lot more sensitive about her feelings. I had failed to give her the traditional strong male influence she desperately needed. I had failed my Ukrainian lady.

    During the next few days, our letters returned to near normal, but I began to put pressure on Oksana to communicate with me off the Ukraine Brides website. Incredibly, I was pushing her hard immediately after I had seriously disappointed her.

    I had been reading some blogs on the internet about Russian dating site scams. In one of the blogs someone said, "If you are talking to this lady only on the dating site and she won't use Skype, Viber, FB, or other sites, there is absolutely no doubt that it is a scam." This sounded reasonable to me. After all, if you say you love someone, why wouldn't you want more direct communication with them?

She was writing several letters a day now and most of them were asking me to change my mind about going to Kyiv. In one of those letters, she said, "My darling, you have my heart in your hands, please don't break it. I am yours, Oksana."

I didn't write a letter for three days. When I did write, I told her I loved her, and I was waiting for her decision about communicating on another site. She ignored my request but told me she was thinking of going to Kyiv without me since she had made her vacation plans.

During this time, Oksana sent me some of her most intimate and romantic letters. I replied to a few of them just to let her know I still cared about her. It was a difficult time, and our relationship could have gone either way. Then on Christmas Eve, she sent me a Christmas picture. She was wearing a sexy Santa Clause dress. She was holding a sign that read, "Merry Christmas to My Man Matt."

First, she had called me Joe and now she was calling me Matt. I could see her in some room in Kharkiv with someone passing these signs to her and taking her picture. If you are writing letters to a lot of men I can see where you can get confused. But matching the picture with the letter is critical—at least it was critical to me.

I immediately sent her a letter that said, "Dear Oksana, thank you for your beautiful picture but my name isn't MATT! I am afraid you have made a fatal mistake."
After I got over the initial shock of the picture, I wrote her a more detailed letter than explained my feelings.

My Dear Oksy,
None of us really believe in magic. We all know that magic tricks are simply tricks. The magician's job is to make certain he keeps the secret of his trick from the audience. Well, now I know your secret, sweetheart. Someone writes a lot of letters to a lot of different people. They hire a lot of beautiful women. They take a lot of pictures. But sometimes, in all the confusion, the wrong letter goes out attached to the wrong picture. Of course, this could easily be prevented by simply looking at the name in the letter and comparing it to the picture. But mistakes do happen. Now I am wondering if it's just you or is it the entire Ukraine Brides site. I don't know but I am going to try to find that out.
There is one other thing; it isn't nice to play with other people's hearts. In fact, it's downright cruel.
Happy Holidays!
Not Matt!

Oksana's reply was immediate.

My Lovely Man!
Matt? I meant Mate, my dear! Who is Matt? Is that the name of your new girlfriend?
Sorry my dear, my English isn't very good. I hope one day you will be able to help me with it. I was just trying to make

a Christmas surprise for you. I didn't mean for it to be this kind of surprise!
I wish you a warm and wonderful Christmas Eve, my dear.
With kisses and hugs,
Oksana"

Yes, it was a lame response. But what can you say when you have been caught red handed? She even sent an additional letter that was even worse than this one. She was confused and she was trying to confuse me. It must have worked because, despite my threats, I kept replying to her letters. Previously I mentioned that there would be things in my story that are difficult to believe. This is one of those things.

Chapter Thirty-One

After Christmas, I was still trying to deal with the Matt problem, but we were writing letters almost every day. Oksana continued to tell me she was booking her train trip to Kyiv, and she wanted me to meet her there. I was telling her I likely wasn't coming to Kyiv. This went on almost every day until about two days before she was to leave for Kyiv. On January 11, 2016, I sent this letter:

My Dear Oksana,
When I am able to get your personal information, we can communicate much better on the internet. As I have already told you, we will have to do this before we actually meet. I will need your full name and passport number to purchase your airline tickets. That is required. And I want to tell you now that I will not be coming to Kyiv this week. But I want to be with you soon. How long do you think it will be before you can take some time off again? I hope you are staying warm. I saw where it is going to get bitterly cold there in a few days.
I love you, Oksy.

Oksana went forward with her Kyiv plans. She wrote,

My Dear,
I would like to remind you that I am going to Kyiv tonight. You are the reason I will be going. You are the reason I will be traveling a long distance by train in frost and snow after

working all day. There will be no one there for me to hold. There will be no lover. There will no soulmate.
I am going to Kyiv. This is the city where you agreed to meet me. Now I am going with a crying soul!
Oksy

The next day I sent Oksana a letter and told her I had just about given up on us because she refused to give me her contact information. I was paying five dollars for every letter I sent and there were a lot of better ways to keep in touch. There was something wrong here, but I couldn't quite figure it out. She was a smart woman who was acting dumb for some reason. She was willing to travel to Kyiv to meet me, but she hung on to a dating website that could disconnect us at any time and for any reason. If Ukraine Brides decided, we had violated some policy I would likely never see or hear from Oksana again. No doubt she knew this. Why would she be willing to take such an inordinate risk? I kept thinking about the internet blog that warned against this kind of thing. It had stated, "100% scam."
I didn't contact Oksana for five days. It was five days of hell because she sent me several letters every day.
   Here is a typical letter:

My Dearest,
I just can't stop thinking of you my MAN! What are you thinking at this moment?" What are your honest feelings when you think about me and a future together? Do you believe what we have is real or just a dream that will never come true? Well, I have a surprise for you. If you are honest with me, and you are the man you say you are, I believe we

will be happy together, not for one day or several weeks, but for our lifetime!
Oksy
On January 17, she wrote:

My Honey!
All I can do is catch you in my dreams. Every night I see you here with me. I feel your hand on my head and I hear your heart beating when I lay my head on your chest.
You are so special to me my dear. When will you return to me? Please don't leave me! I need YOU!!!!!!
I'M missing you so much.
Oksana
I could take it no longer. So, on January 17, I sent her a letter:
My Oksana!
My Imaginary Lover.
My Oksy.

Today I tried to send you my personal information, but the site would not deliver it to you. The site controls everything we say to each other. When I asked the site for your information, you refused to give it to me and the site kept my $100 request fee. I want to talk to you off of this site. What do you want me to do?
I still think we will meet one day. Maybe we should begin thinking of meeting in spring. What do you think?
I hope you are happy and well.
Yours.

Oksana quickly replied,

Happy and well!!! I will only be happy in your arms darling. You are the one who brought happiness into my life. You are the only one who can make me happy sweetheart. I even showed your pictures to my sister and brother recently. They asked me if I was just imagining you. My sister asked me, "Oksy, are you going crazy?"

Yes, spring is a good time to meet. It will be just the two of us. I will be in your arms. This is my dream.

Thinking of you,

Oksana

Chapter Thirty-Two

Oksana had agreed to begin planning another meeting for the spring of 2016. But the subject of our letters didn't change much. I was still pressing her to get on the free internet and she was insisting that we wait until we met to exchange contact information. It was a continuing battle that threatened our relationship for months.

On January 21, I sent Oksana a letter. I told her I had met a man who had been to Ukraine more than 30 times. He had married a woman from there and he returned with his wife occasionally. Charles was very complimentary of Ukraine and the people, but he had told me, "You should not agree to meet any woman in Ukraine who will not give you her cellphone number and her other contact information." This sounded logical to me. I had read it on the internet blogs and now it was coming directly from a man with extensive Ukrainian experience.

I didn't write a letter for two days, but Oksy wrote eight or ten times. She finally wrote that she was worried about me because of a terrible storm that was affecting the eastern seaboard of the U.S. She told me she had been following the storm on the internet and was concerned about my safety. On January 23, I sent her a letter and explained that the winter storm was well north of my location and that I was perfectly safe.
While I was communicating with Oksana, I was continuing to date women on the internet. I was beginning to develop some strong feelings for Oksana, but she

was six thousand miles away. When you meet someone special in person, it's not very difficult to begin making changes in your life. A long-distance relationship is very different. I had never met the woman and I might never meet her. It all sounded great, but I had heard of the rumors and read the internet blogs. And there were all of these red flags to consider. In hindsight, I was very confused during this time. I was telling Oksana I loved her while I was dating other women. That was not right. I can only suppose that I was doing an incredible job of compartmentalization. No matter, it was wrong.

The Ukraine Brides site offers a lot of advice for their male users. For example, they tell you to avoid sending expensive gifts to the ladies. They try to screen all of their ladies, but it is impossible to keep up with thousands of women for many different dating agencies. And the process is ripe for fraud. They also recommend that couples meet for a video chat early in the relationship. That is a little difficult because of the language barrier but it is essential. Most couples meet on Skype, but many other sites offer video chatting.

Oksana was very hesitant to meet me on a video chat site. This was another little red flag I noticed waving somewhere in the distance. But the distance was so great and the flag so small I hardly noticed. Come to think of it, I don't believe I ever initiated a video chat with Oksana. She finally agreed to do it but she was always the one initiating the call. There's another little red flag. Maybe I'm color blind. I might have trouble counting as well.

Chapter Thirty-Three

Our messages in late January and throughout February were the usual letters between two people who were in love. When I wrote one letter, Oksana would send five replies. About every other message from her asked me to join her in an onsite chat. These requests were usually just tacked on to the end of her letters. But on February 3, 2016, she sent me a detailed plea for more letters.

Good morning, my darling!
The way we start our day is the way we will spend it. You see how important it is to wake up in a good mood and with nice emotions? I know one very effective method for doing that. Listen to me here!
To wake up easily, we need to know something good is waiting for us in the morning. This special day you can have every day, my dear. You just need to find me in chat and let me brighten your day. If you can't join me in chat, just write to me when you first open your eyes and while you are still in bed. Let's make it a tradition!
Sincerely,
Oksana

Since Oksana had refused to allow the site to give me her contact information, I had tried to restrict my writing to one letter a day. Whether the letter was ten words long or five hundred words, it didn't matter. The cost was the same—five dollars. Of course, Oksana knew this and always encouraged me to write her more often. On February 11, she wrote:

Honey,
We are far apart but we can easily break the distance between us by starting our days together and by keeping in touch during the day. It would be so sweet to receive a short reminder that a loving person remembered you. During the day we have so many thoughts. So, why collect them all in a single letter? Please just log in the chat room and let me tell you about me. It is evening here. I want to remind you that you are in my thoughts. I don't think I will be able to sleep without news from you.
Am I asking too much?
Your Oksy

Then, on Valentine's Day, February 14, Oksana dropped another bomb.

Hello My Dear,
Are you drinking champagne alone on this special day? Are you online? I want to know you better, my man Ken. Other men are just not interesting to me.
I wonder how you are spending your time there. What places do you visit? Who do you talk to? I'm a curious Ukraine lady! I am talking to you, sweetheart! Do you hear me?
Kisses, always,
Oksy

Yes, I am keeping up. First, there was Joe. Second, there was Matt. Now, there was Ken. I wasn't getting used to it. Every time it happened it was a kick in the stomach.

The only way to explain my tolerating this is to say that I had accepted the fact that she was earning money working for Ukraine Brides. The people in Ukraine are desperate and they will do just about anything to make ends meet. A single woman in Ukraine has an especially difficult time. It's a weak reason, but it is the best I can do at the moment. I think I will have another excuse soon. I'm working on it.

Chapter Thirty-Four

Oksana's requests for letters and chats, coupled with her calling me by other men's names, had reduced my letter writing to less than once a day. She might write ten or twelve letters before I replied. She was incredibly patient when I didn't write for a few days. She complained, of course, but she never once threatened to stop writing me. In retrospect, I see that it had less to do with how much she loved me and much more to do with her income from Ukraine Brides. And, of course, Ukraine Brides was writing a lot of the letters for her.

Around February 20, Oksana began to remind me of her upcoming birthday on February 23. She wasn't subtle. She sent messages like, "I hope to talk with you soon. Are you thinking about my great day?" And "What should your lady expect on her SPECIAL day?"

Oksana and her friend Tanya had gone to Kyiv for her birthday trip. Ukraine Brides had done a great job of finding her and delivering a dozen roses on her birthday. As I have mentioned, gifts—however small—are hugely important to Ukrainian women. Unfortunately, not giving gifts has the equal and opposite effect. But on this day, I had done well. Oksana was excited and happy.

My Wonderful Sweetheart!
OH, MY MAN! If you only knew how much I'd like to spend this special day with you. Hooray!!!! The dream has come true, my honey!
I am so glad you are with me darling!

Tanya and I went to a sweetshop and bought some chocolates. Tonight we are going to a nice cozy restaurant and have my birthday dinner. Do you want to join us, honey? Thank you for your most important place in my life and thank you for my special gift on my special day.
Kisses

My simple gift had created a delightful atmosphere in our somewhat troubled relationship, and I was caught up in the moment. I sent her a quick reply.

My Dearest Oksana,
I saw your sweet smiling face with your birthday roses. What a special pleasure. I am happy you like the flowers. I haven't sent roses in several years. I guess I should have.
You might be right about this site. They did a good job of delivering your flowers and the pictures they sent me were much more than I expected.
I am sending you a picture I just took in the gym. It's a picture of the only tattoo I have anywhere on my body. I got it yesterday! The red heart in the middle is my heart. I am giving it to you. Please take good care of it.
Yours, always. All ways!

Oksana and I had certainly had our issues, but now things had settled down and we were on our way. It is truly amazing how a relationship between two people can improve when one of the parties, for whatever reason, chooses to ignore the bizarre actions of the other.

I can hear my father again, "Son, you traded for it."

Chapter Thirty-Five

February quietly became March, and Oksana and I settled into a pattern of intimate love letters. We had our occasional quarrels, but these were overcome by passionate words of love. She continued her constant requests for letters, but I had gotten used to this by now. It was just background noise and I ignored it.

We had to delay our Kyiv meeting plans. Oksana had taken off from work several times recently and her boss had told her it would be June before she could take another vacation. This sounded reasonable to me so we began to talk about meeting in late June. I was also thinking the weather would be much better at that time. Kyiv is at about the same latitude as Calgary, Canada, and I knew spring arrive late.

It was along about this time when I began to notice some of Oksana's letters were repeats of previous letters. Like someone going insane, she was telling me the same stories over and over again. But this wasn't because she was losing her mind. It was likely because she was using form letters from Ukraine Brides.

Of course, the introductions and closings were personalized but sandwiched in between were some oddly familiar stories. For some reason this didn't seem to bother me very much.

Then, on March 31, Oksana sent me a very interesting letter.

Good evening, my dear, from the cold city of Kharkov.

Someone has said love is blind. What can you say about this? Does it mean that when we fall in love we don't see the real situation? We see only those things which attract us to the other person and do not see the flaws? We lose our ability to think rationally when we are under the spell of love?
How is this possible? How do you feel about this?
Please give this some thought and tell me what you think.
Hugs.
Oksy

Of course, I knew I was "under the spell of love." But I just didn't see that as a bad thing. It's love; it's not supposed to be rational. But I was very surprised that she had broached the subject. I was thinking it must be some kind of reverse psychology. Perhaps if she brought up the subject, I might be more comfortable with my doubts and concerns.

Chapter Thirty-Six

Another subject that kept rearing its ugly head was my alleged fear of going to Ukraine. Oksana kept mentioning that my fears had kept me from going to Kyiv in January and that was the reason I had left her there alone in the cold. I had ignored these comments because I knew where the conversation would end, and it wasn't a pleasant place.

However, when she sent me a letter on April 24, I could take it no longer.

Hello My Dear,
I am getting so excited about our trip! When you purchase your tickets please send a picture of them to me. I am sure you remember my last January trip to Kyiv! Yes, that time when you promised to meet me and you didn't show up.
And, why did you decide to do all of this so far in advance? Why so fast, honey?
I see you have chosen the Opera Hotel. That is a very nice hotel and it is very convenient to the subway and to shopping. But why don't you like the apartments. Are you afraid? Again?
I am a bit shocked.
Oksana

Oksana had accused me of being afraid of the soldiers on the streets, the Ukrainian police, the war in eastern Ukraine, and the Ukraine Mafia. Now she was adding my fear of apartments for some obscure reason.

I understand people can get used to the sound of gunfire in the street and the rumble of distant bombs. I think you would have to be a damned fool not to be cautious when traveling to a weak third-world country that is at war with a superpower with an unpredictable leader. Hell, I think you might be a damned fool for traveling there anyway.

Truth be told, I don't know if Ukraine is a third-world country. I know this is a very disparaging remark about a country and the people of Ukraine are very sensitive about it. But my definition of "third-world" is any country where you can't drink the water. I once told a Ukrainian woman in the U.S. this and she replied, "You are wrong. You can drink the water in Kyiv. You just have to be sure it comes from a bottle!" LOL.

In any event, I had heard just about all I wanted to hear on the various subjects, and I sent Oksana a letter expressing my thoughts.

My Dearest Oksana,
First, I want to tell you how much I care about you. I am happy you are in my life. I very much look forward to meeting you in Kyiv.
Now, you have said you want to know more about me. Well, I am going to tell you a few things about me in this letter.
I just returned from a motorcycle ride with some friends. I ride a Harley Davidson Vrod. Its top speed is about 240 km/hour. I am not afraid of much and I, like most men, don't appreciate being accused of being afraid. So, please stop doing that.

I have traveled to 25 countries including Russia, Peru, Cuba, and Mexico. I wasn't afraid in those countries and I won't be afraid in Ukraine.

Next, I am sorry you were alone in Kyiv in January. But I told you in advance that I would not be able to make the trip. It was your choice to go there without me, so please stop mentioning this every few days.

I have been doing this internet dating thing for over a year. I have a few rules about this activity. One of them is I never text or message anyone for more than three days without meeting them. I have been chatting with you for over six months! Why? It is because you are special. So, I broke my rule for you.

I am moving "so fast" because I will save a lot of money by booking everything early.

Finally, I don't allow other people to book accommodations for me, because if I make a mistake and pick a bad hotel, I have no one to blame but myself. I stay in nice hotels because that is a big part of the trip for me.

I hope this helps you understand a little more about me and I hope we won't need to discuss these issues again.

Yours

All ways.

Oksana replied with some meandering letter about the selection of apartments in Kyiv and the cost savings. Then she continued to mention being alone in Kyiv in January. I assume she read my letter, but it didn't soak in.

However, her letters then took on a more romantic tone. I believe this was because of the traditional Ukrainian values I had heard so much about. I had been firm and put my foot down. I had made a decision and the woman had agreed. That didn't mean she wasn't going to change her mind, but at least she was trying to follow the rules.

Two days later, she wrote:

My Sweet Dreamer,
You make my heart beat faster with each letter, darling! I just imagine warm, special days and evenings in Kyiv.
How do you like big cities? You are used to calm mountains and Veuve Cliquot on the back porch.
I feel something new and special you have brought into my life. I can't imagine how I lived before meeting you.
I want to feel you close to me and see you for real and make our plans for our future together my dear. Let's make our dreams come true!
Oksana

Yes, very romantic. I was touched. Looking back, I think her heart was beating faster because she could hear the Ukraine Brides' cash register ringing in her head.

Chapter Thirty-Seven

There were times when I wondered if Oksana read my letters. If she did, she certainly wasn't honoring my requests. In one of her letters, she delivered a double whammy. On April 28, she wrote:

My Love,
So, are you really getting ready for our trip, sweetheart? Have you decided on the hotel? Or maybe we could get an apartment in the city centre? I am just worrying about you so much and I want you to feel comfortable darling.
Hugs,
Oksana
PS: I was just wondering why you didn't come in January to Ukraine. Were you really afraid?

I was beginning to think that Russian women just gave lip service to traditional values. It occurred to me that it might all be bullshit.

Most of Oksana's letters at the end of April and the beginning of May were informing me about her life in Ukraine. There was almost always some mention of her love for me and a gentle reminder to keep the cards and letters coming. In a short letter dated May 9, she wrote:

My Dear,
First I want to thank you for your patience with me, darling. I know you will be there this time in Kyiv, my dearest. You can be sure that I will also be there. We have grown so close

during these months together. Now it is so hard for me to wake up if I don't see even a short letter from you in the morning.
I am truly ready to change my life. Now it ALL depends on you, darling. Please give us a chance. Will you?
I want to see you in chat today!
Oksana

The nudges are subtle, but they are unmistakably there. She reminded me I wasn't there for her in January, she wasn't sure I would be there in June, and she wanted to see more letters. And she and Ukraine Brides wanted more income.

I completely understood her concern about my being in Kyiv in June. It was a huge commitment. I had the same concerns about her. I could just imagine traveling over 6,000 miles to meet someone and they simply don't show up. What do you do? Get the next flight back home? Try to find someone else? It wasn't an easy question to answer. For example, the airfare to Kyiv is a bargain. If you change your plans, however, the airlines will screw you to the wall. I once tried to delay my departure from Kyiv by three days. Expedia quoted me a price of $2,500. My original round-trip ticket was only $1,200 and the airline wanted to charge me more than twice that amount for a one-way ticket. I finally called Delta Airlines and told them I was sick, and they needed to be sure my seat was near a restroom. They quickly delayed my departure and charged me "only" $600 for the change.

I hope the recent debacle with United Airlines will encourage all airline companies to treat the customer with a little more respect and consideration. I am not optimistic.

Chapter Thirty-Eight

I had asked Ukraine Brides to help with some of the details of our upcoming trip to Kyiv. On May 9, they sent me an email requesting some detailed information that would be required before meeting with Oksana. An International Marriage Broker Act (IMBRA) form had to be completed and the time and date of our meeting had to be set. They also gave me the contact information for Vlada, our translator.

I thought it was a little strange that I was receiving the contact information for the translator so quickly while I had not been able to get Oksana's information for seven months. Of course, this was not the fault of the website. Oksana had simply refused to give it to me because she was making a living receiving letters.

Here is the last paragraph of the email I received from Ukraine Brides:

We have noticed that you will have a meeting with the lady with username Woman_For_Life and you have zero minutes in a video chat.
Due to our experience, we are informing you that men who come to Ukraine to meet a lady after correspondence, without ever seeing them in a video chat, can be disappointed after the meeting. The lady can also be disappointed. The reason for this is they have formed an impression about each other from pictures and photos which can be different from reality.

So, we insist that you hold a video chat with the lady before the trip. We also recommend that you ask her all of the questions you need to ask her during this chat.

A lot has been written about the scams that are prevalent on Russian dating sites. Most of it is likely true. But this advice from Ukraine Brides was right on target. A picture is worth a thousand words, but they do lie. It is much more difficult to fake a live video than it is to fake a photograph. Trust me. I am the seasoned expert here.

I want to make it very clear that Oksana had not refused to have a video chat. She had a lot of difficulty borrowing a camera that would work with her PC and we had had a hard time coordinating our video chat and working out the logistics.

When we finally did the video chat it didn't go well. We had a bad internet connection and Oksana was had some problems with her camera. But the chat had met the requirement of Ukraine Brides and I had been able to see and hear Oksana. Her unforgettable smile was beautiful and genuine, but her English was very poor.

This surprised me because she had made a decision to come to America a long time ago and we had been chatting for months. I wondered why she had not been taking English lessons to prepare herself for her future. It was another red flag. This one was so small I didn't even see it at the time.

After the video chat, Oksana sent me a short letter with her thoughts.

Sweetheart,

Have you seen on the site how many times I have nudged you darling? I am trying to get your attention!
I know the internet connection was not so good, dear. But we saw each other and what could be better, darling? We both saw real positive emotions in each other's eyes! Do you agree?
Oksana

I replied to her immediately.
My Dearest Oksana,
Thank you for your four letters! Yes, I also saw your nudges. I think we were both a little disappointed in the quality of the video chat but the results were great. I could see the excitement and happiness in your eyes and that made it all worthwhile.
I am also excited and happy. I think about our meeting in Kyiv many times throughout each day. I can't wait to see if this is going to work for us. I certainly hope it does.
Always. All ways!

After the video chat, I felt much better about our relationship and our chances of overcoming incredible odds. But the closer it got to our meeting the more nervous both of us became.

Chapter Thirty-Nine

Oksana and I were candid about our concerns that one of us would not make it to Kyiv. I think we may have been too candid. It began to sound like we didn't trust each other. I should have been more patient, and she should have tried to refrain from mentioning the January trip I had missed.

On May 28, Oksana sent me another rambling letter.

My Romantic Planner,
I am at my parent's house today. I really like it here.
So, we are meeting on Saturday, June 25, in the afternoon, at 15:00 Kyiv time. Don't worry, I will find the hotel.
You have asked me about my plan. My plan is to stay with you. What is your plan?
I plan to arrive on Thursday evening. I will need some time to rest up and get ready to see you!
Do you still have doubts about my arrival in Kyiv?
You have done a great job selecting the hotel. Well done!
I will be there. Will you be there?
Oksana

Some of her letters weren't rambling. Some of them got directly to the main point.

My Dear,
I am a busy girl but today I rest.
Please tell me why you don't like to write letters. Maybe you need a pause before our meeting. Maybe you just don't like

to write them? So, if you need a little pause before the real meeting, just tell me. Ok?
Maybe your friends have told you again it's not safe to fly to Ukraine? Hmmmmm.
Maybe we need to chat more if you don't like to write letters.
Oksana

This was a blatant ad for Ukraine Brides, et al. At this point Oksana was sending a half dozen letters a day. If I had replied to every one of these letters it would have cost me around $200 a week. That is about the average monthly income for a Ukrainian public employee.

The closer we got to our meeting, the less romantic the letters became. Of course, we had to discuss logistics, but there was something else that affected the tone of our messages to each other. It must have been that we were both a little anxious about the meeting. We were both afraid something would happen to keep us apart. And there were a lot of things that could have happened.

Around the middle of June, just days before our meeting, we were at one of the low points in our relationship. Oksana's letters were full of complaints about the weather, her job, the food, the paperwork for our meeting, and various other problems she was having at the time. In one of her letters, she even mentioned that she hated to leave her mother for a week. It got so bad I wrote this letter to her on June 18:

My Dearest Oksana,
Months ago I read in your profile on the site that there was a huge void in your life. You had no one to give your love to.

You were looking for your one and only. You asked me if I agreed with you. Well, I did agree with you and I have told you many times I want to fill that void.
Early in our conversations you were very positive about us. Lately, however, you have become less passionate about us and now you tell me you don't want to leave your mother next week!
I am excited about our meeting next week. I will be there. I don't know if you will be there or not. And, if you are there, I am now confused about what you want. Do you know what you want?
I love you, Oksy, but I don't think you are sure what you are looking for. I hope you will be able to decide soon.
Yours always

Oksana replied, but her letter didn't help much. She told me she knew what she wanted but she didn't tell me what it was. She also repeated her accusation that I had left her alone in Kyiv in January. I didn't even refute this because it was doing no good.

The day my flight left Birmingham; Oksana sent me a confusing letter. She was complaining about a heat wave they were having in Kharkiv. I think the temperature was in the low eighties. But the letter also suggested that she was nervous and naïve about traveling.

Hello My Dear,
I am afraid to fly. I hope you aren't afraid of flying.
It is very hot outside here in Kharkiv. I hope it isn't this hot in the train to Kyiv. Will your airplane have good air conditioning? I hope you will be comfortable.

I see you are coming through Amsterdam. That is a big and well-known city.
I hope it won't be so hot in Kyiv. When I was on the job our air conditioner was broken. It will be really hot in Kyiv. I hope you brought a light suit.
I hope you are prepared for Ukraine service, dear. It's not like American service. To us, America is like another planet!
Hugs,
Oksana

The temperature outside at 37,000 feet is about -56 degrees centigrade. The aircraft air conditioning system will have to heat the air for passengers to survive. Oksana's letters during this period were just an introduction to one of her critical issues. She was a complainer. If something didn't go according to her expectations, she would not let it go. It could be something as simple as coffee being too hot or too cold. Of course, it could be something much more important. In the beginning, I thought her complaints were kind of cute. Later they would become very annoying. This was beginning to feel like a normal relationship.

Chapter Forty

Oksana graduated from college with a degree in accounting. She said she worked in the "banking sphere." The employment situation in Ukraine is very complicated. It is also very difficult to relate to. Since her family lived in a rural area south of Kharkiv she was having a difficult time with her career. She told me that residents of Kharkiv were treated much better than outsiders. She wasn't making a lot of progress.

And, in despite her education, she was not earning much money. The average worker in the private sector in Ukraine makes around 7,500 hryvnias a month. That's less than $300 US dollars. The average government worker earns even less. Oksana never asked me for money. If she had asked, I would have given it to her. She did get some help from her parents, which she gladly accepted. I thought it was a little strange for a college-educated thirty-six-year-old woman to need financial help from her parents, but in Ukraine, it's a necessity. You can't live on $300 a month.

When Oksana agreed to meet me in Kyiv, I asked her if she was going to be able to take off from work for a week. She told me she had someone who could substitute for her for the week. That seemed reasonable to me. I asked if she had enough money for the trip and she said she did. I told her I would reimburse her when she arrived in Kyiv.

I began to firm up the flights and hotels and she began to make her travel arrangements. We decided on the week of June 19, 2016. I booked a room at the Opera Hotel in Kyiv on Hotels.com and booked my flight to Kyiv through Expedia.com. The flight from Birmingham to Kyiv goes through Atlanta and either Paris or Amsterdam. I chose Amsterdam because I hate Charles de Gaulle airport. It has to be the most confusing airport in the world. I was surprised by how inexpensive it was to fly for so many hours.

When my friends and family discovered I was going to Ukraine, the proverbial shit hit the fan. Everyone thought I was kidding. Then they thought I had completely lost my mind. I knew a little about what was going on in the world and it didn't seem like that big a deal. But since there was so much concern for my safety and mental stability, I decided to do some further research online.

Tensions had indeed increased in recent months in the area. Russia was sending troops into Ukraine and had taken over two airports in the eastern area. Sporadic clashes continued in parts of Donetsk and Luhansk, where pro-Russian rebels faced Ukrainian government troops. In many cases, families were divided by political unrest. My loved ones were correct; times were not good for a Ukraine vacation. But I wasn't going on vacation. I was going to meet someone to marry.

It takes about 20 hours to fly from Birmingham, Alabama to Kyiv, Ukraine. I don't mind flying for a few hours but the flight from Atlanta to Amsterdam is about nine hours. I am claustrophobic and the seats were jammed in there pretty tight. I discovered my fear of close places when I climbed into an MRI machine a few months before my trip. I had to get out of the machine and get some Valium before completing the test.

So, when I was in my doctor's office for my annual physical, I told him about my MRI experience and asked him if he would prescribe some Valium for me to use on my long airplane ride. He thought it was a good idea and gave me a prescription for 30 tablets. I was surprised because he had prescribed only one tablet for my MRI issues.

The Valium worked wonders. I had tried Ambien several times and it didn't work for me. The Valium did exactly what it was supposed to do. On one subsequent flight from Kyiv to Amsterdam, the flight attendant had to awaken me to get me off the plane. The flight was on Ukraine International Airlines. I had taken a whole tablet and swallowed it with a glass of wine. Mixing drugs, especially with alcohol, can be dangerous but this combination was perfect.

Kyiv is eight hours ahead of Birmingham. I boarded the Delta flight in Birmingham around the middle of the morning and I was in Kyiv around the middle of the afternoon the next day. Delta has partnerships with Air France and KLM. The flights from Atlanta to Amsterdam and from Amsterdam to Kyiv were on KLM flights. I love KLM and they do a good job making your flight as enjoyable as possible. But the ordeal takes 20 hours and there is no way to eliminate this wear and tear on your mind and body.

Chapter Forty-One

Crossing the border into a third-world country can be intimidating. You never know what to expect from border control agents. I completely understand the scrutiny that must be given to visitors, but the way some people are treated is unnecessary. I know these people have a lot of latitudes and they are police officers, so I treat them with a lot of respect just as I do all police officers.

Various internet blogs warn visitors to Ukraine of potential shakedowns by the authorities. They warn about extortion from traffic police, and they specifically mention border officials. During my five visits to Kyiv over the seven months, I was never once approached for a bribe. The police were aloof and not very cordial, but they didn't give me any problems.

Ukraine Brides had arranged for a taxi to pick me up at the airport. I saw a man holding a sign with my name on it and I followed him to his cab. It's about a forty-five-minute cab ride from Boryspil International Airport to downtown Kyiv. The trip goes through some depressed areas. There are dilapidated high rises where people who work downtown live. There are about two and a half million people in Kyiv and most of them live in these very small flats on the outskirts of the city. The flats downtown are more or less for the more affluent residents.

The billboards and street signs are, of course, all in Russian. The Russian alphabet has almost nothing in common with the English alphabet. The taxi driver spoke very little English. The result was that I was now virtually illiterate. The only thing I understood was the billboards advertising monthly rental rates for the flats. I knew the Ukrainian hryvnia was equal to about $.04. So a quote of 6,250 hryvnias was about $250. It is surprising how quickly you pick up some of the Russian language when you must communicate to survive. That is the reason a foreign language is so much easier to learn if you are in that country. But the Russian language is harsh, and it is difficult to learn under any circumstances. It might be as difficult to learn as English.

The Opera Hotel had an outstanding rating on Hotels.com. On the ride from the airport, I was wondering if the site graded on the curve. They don't. The Opera Hotel is comparable to any of the fine hotels in the world. The staff speaks English; they are very cordial and are very friendly once you get to know them. And I got to know them pretty well during my almost 60 days there over seven months. Eventually, I would begin to feel like a resident. I tipped well, returned their kindness, and they treated me like a king.

The Opera Hotel in Kyiv

Chapter Forty-Two

The Ukraine Brides website offers some very helpful guidelines regarding the messaging and meeting process. They take care of the details. But there is no guidance regarding the number of women you should meet on a visit. That is entirely up to the individual. I would recommend they add that to the guidelines. I had originally considered meeting five or six different ladies. After all, I was flying 6,000 miles and spending a lot of money. Again, what was I going to do in Kyiv if I chose to meet one lady and she didn't show? Fortunately, I reduced that number from five or six to two. As it turned out, that was one too many.

    I arrived a full 24 hours before my first meeting. That was fortunate because it took me that long to somewhat adjust to the eight-hour time change. When I arrived, I was tired from the trip? But my room was very comfortable, and I slept like a baby.

    I got up the following morning and went down to the lobby for a cup of coffee. The Opera Hotel has a small restaurant on the street level that has some tables out on the sidewalk. The weather was beautiful, so I asked for an outside table. Even here there were white tablecloths and linen napkins. I ordered a cup of American coffee and a croissant. I was in for a surprise. It was the best coffee I had ever tasted. Even the American version was thick and robust. At the time, I rarely drank anything but decaf coffee. I made an exception every time I was in Kyiv.

The sidewalk café at the Opera Hotel in Kyiv

    When Ukrainian women walk out the door of their flat, they are ready to go anywhere. They spend a lot of time with their makeup and their hair. You won't see a woman who has quickly brushed her hair and thrown on a sweat suit on the streets of Kyiv. While I was having breakfast, I couldn't help but notice a lovely young woman walking down the street in front of the hotel. She knew she was beautiful. I could tell by the way she carried herself. She was the personification of sexy. I also couldn't help noticing the other men at the café didn't pay any attention to her. I guess you can get accustomed to anything. But I was not accustomed yet. As she passed the café, she looked me right in the eyes and smiled. I knew I was in the right place.

My first meeting was at 1:00 p.m. at the hotel. I had a few hours to kill so I walked up the street toward the National Opera of Ukraine. Opera is a big deal in Kyiv and this building is magnificent. I then took a left on a street I couldn't pronounce and walked a few blocks to Saint Sophia's Cathedral. It was easy to locate. It has a gold dome, and the cathedral is an outstanding architectural monument. While standing in front of Saint Sophia's, you can see Saint Michael's Golden-Domed Monastery just two blocks away.

The Cathedral of St. Sophia in Kyiv

Kyiv is home to magnificent churches and government buildings, but I couldn't help but think how ridiculous it was to spend all of this money on buildings when most of the people were so poor. This happens all over the world. It seems to me that the poorer the people, the larger the churches. I am sure it's just my philosophical issues.

I had been walking for a couple of hours and it was time to head back to the hotel and get ready for my meeting. I had walked the adjacent and opposite sides of a triangle. I decided to take a shortcut back along the hypotenuse. That wasn't a good idea. Most of the streets in Kyiv aren't laid out at right angles. And the street signs are in Russian. I have a good sense of direction, but I soon got lost in the maze. I decided to try to get a map on my cellphone. When I opened the navigation area, Google popped up. I decided to type in "Opera Hotel, Kyiv." Siri immediately replied, "Continue walking 200 yards, take a left, and your destination will be 100 yards on your right." I was only 300 yards from my hotel, and I was lost. From that moment on, whenever I walked around Kyiv, Google was my first thought.

I arrived at the hotel in plenty of time to get a good shower, have a glass of wine, and wait for my first lady of Ukraine. I have rarely traveled alone. I am usually with someone special or with a group of friends. This experience was new and exciting. I was feeling great about where I was and what was about to happen.

Chapter Forty-Two

My meeting with Oksana was not scheduled until the next day. Today I was meeting with a thirty-five-year-old Ukrainian woman with long black hair. She was an attorney in Kyiv. Her name was Ludmilla, but she wanted me to call her Mila.

I want to press the pause button here and try to explain something that I am certain is sounding strange. Again, here I am telling Oksana I love her while communicating with another woman. Please keep in mind that I have never met Oksana. Also, that she has addressed me by four different names. She has received income for seven months from Ukraine Brides and she is worried about missing her mother while meeting with me in Kyiv. Add 6,000 miles and months of anxiety and the result is Mila.

Mila and I had been messaging on Ukraine Brides for a couple of months. This woman was strikingly beautiful even by Ukrainian standards. Her pictures were amazing. Her main photograph on the site was of her holding a violin. She was truly one of the most beautiful women I had ever seen. She had posted a video on the site of her walking by a lake and stopping to feed the ducks. She was simply breathtaking.

I was sitting in the lobby of the Opera Hotel when Mila and the translator walked in. You never know what to expect when you first meet someone from any site. Pictures can be beautiful but sometimes they don't resemble the real person. But there was no mistaking this woman for anyone else. She was just as beautiful in person as in her pictures. I guess I was staring because she flashed a knowing smile immediately. She reached out her hand with her palm down. There was no other choice but to kiss it.

We sat down on one of the French provincial sofas in the hotel lobby and a waitress brought us each a glass of Ukrainian chardonnay. This wine is surprisingly good, and I drank it almost every day when I was in Kyiv. The translator sat down across from us. Mila spoke a little English. I learned to speak a little Russian later on but at this time I knew about a dozen words—not an impressive vocabulary.

Ukraine Brides provides some excellent translators. The two I met were lovely ladies themselves. They were also friendly and sociable. Irina was an English teacher in Kyiv, so her English was excellent.

We talked for about thirty minutes, and I asked Mila if she wanted to get something to eat. She said she was hungry, so we went upstairs to the main restaurant for a late lunch. The food at the Opera Hotel is excellent and the service is impeccable. We drank another glass of the chardonnay with our meal and chatted. Mila volunteered to take me on a tour of a historic monastery in town and Irina agreed to come with us. Immediately after lunch, I asked the concierge to get us a taxi and we left for the monastery. It was another beautiful day in Kyiv.

The monastery was old and interesting. We walked around for a couple of hours. Kyiv is a hilly city and after two hours I was about done. There was a little coffee shop just outside the gate of the monastery. We drank a cup of the wonderful Ukrainian coffee and headed back to the hotel. I paid Irina and we told her goodbye. Mila wanted to go home and freshen up. She asked me if I wanted her to come back later and I said of course.

About two hours later Mila sent me a message on Viber that she was on her way. She wanted to go out to eat at a restaurant called Vino e Cucina. I think that is Italian for wine and meat. The name told me they had their priorities straight. The restaurant was a ten- minute taxi ride from the hotel. She knew her way around the city and she had taken us to a world-class restaurant. We chose a table outside and I ordered a bottle of good French white wine because we had decided we were eating the fish. The meal was delicious. The restaurant is owned by a Ukrainian company called The Family. And I believed it. The place had a mafia feel to it. I based this opinion on my extensive mafia movie experience.

The meal was wonderful, and Mila was a perfect lady. Her English was much better than my Russian and we were able to communicate well most of the time. When we had problems, we simply used the Google translate application on our cellphones. It sounds difficult but, after a while, it becomes second nature. So far, I loved the city, the women, the wine, and the food. Is life great or what?

Chapter Forty-Three

When we had finished dinner at Vino e Cucina we took a cab back to the Opera Hotel. When we arrived at the hotel, I asked Mila if she would like to come inside for a drink. She told me she needed to go home and get to bed because she had to go in to work the next morning. Before I got out of the cab, I leaned over to kiss her goodnight. She turned her head and my kiss landed on her cheek, just as she had planned.
Everything had gone perfectly with Mila, but I was a little disappointed that she wasn't a little more attracted to me. I know we had just met but it is a long way to Kyiv, and I thought the affection curve should be a litter steeper.

Mila told me she would see me the next day after she finished with her work. I knew then that I wasn't going to be able to meet with her the next day, but I just couldn't tell her there in the cab after such a pleasant day. When I got to my room, I sent her a Viber message. I told her that I had previously arranged a meeting with another lady the following day. I explained why. She said she understood, but I knew better.

I told her that I simply could not change the meeting with the other lady. I explained that she was traveling a long way to Kyiv to meet me, and it would not be the right thing to do. I asked her if I could text her and make plans for the day after tomorrow. I didn't expect her to say yes, but she did. I was hoping everything would go as planned with Oksana, but I certainly had no assurance of that. As I mentioned earlier, I had created a difficult situation. It could have been unimaginably worse if I had added a few more women to the mix. It seems that is always the case. A friend who was going through a particularly difficult time once told me a man's happiness is inversely proportioned to the number of women he has in his life. Yes, I know that is sexist.

Chapter Forty-Four

The next morning, I woke up late. My internal clock had not yet adjusted to the time difference, but I was looking forward to the coffee at the sidewalk café downstairs. The waiter recognized me and asked if I wanted my usual. The weather in Kyiv in June is just about perfect. I was surprised there weren't more people eating outside.

I was excited about meeting Oksana. She was the reason I had come to Kyiv. Sadly, Mila had been my backup plan. I felt bad about this, but I think it would have been inordinately risky not to have had one. Long-distance romance is not a game of perfect.

Oksana's train was scheduled to arrive in the middle of the afternoon, and it was already around noon. I had a couple of hours to kill so I went to the gym on the second floor of the hotel for a workout. I work out every other day and I was missing the endorphins.

Around 3:00 p.m. I went down to the hotel lobby and ordered a glass of chardonnay and waited for Oksana. She had still not given me her contact information so I had no idea if she would be on time or if she would show up at all. When I saw her walking through the front doors of the hotel with the translator, I could hardly believe we had pulled this off. But there she was. She was exactly as I had envisioned.

Oksana didn't walk across the lobby of the hotel; she ran. I was hoping for a hug. I was surprised when she jumped into my arms in the lobby of the Opera Hotel. This is a swanky place, and the people were a little astounded at this sight. I was so surprised I almost lost my balance. Now that would have been a spectacle.

Oksana introduced me to Vlada, our translator. She was an attractive woman in her early thirties who spoke nearly perfect English. Oksana was carrying a small gift box. You don't meet someone for the first time in Ukraine without a small gift. It is considered a social blunder and it isn't quickly forgotten. I had brought Oksana a box of nice chocolates, but they were in the room. I should have had them with me in the lobby. It was the first of many issues related to our cultural differences.

I asked if they would like a glass of chardonnay and they both accepted. The waitress was smiling when she brought the wine along with some potato chips and nuts. Oksana sat very near me and put her hand on mine. All of the reservations that had accumulated over the past few months quickly disappeared and I was in Heaven. In just a few minutes, I thought all of the trepidation, logistics, misunderstandings, and other issues were nothing. It had all been worth it. Oksana and I were together and would likely be together forever. Eight months of messaging had been worth it. My dreams had come true. I can't ever remember being happier than I was at that moment.

It had been a long train ride, but Oksana looked as fresh as a daisy. Her hair, her nails, her dress, her scent, everything, was perfect. She quickly told me she was hungry. I appreciated her candor. We went to the restaurant upstairs and ordered some food. Vlada was helping us communicate but we didn't need much help understanding each other.

We took our time with the meal. The main hotel restaurant is very comfortable and inviting. There was a combination of chairs and sofas and there weren't many other people eating at this time of day. Young Ukrainian women with older men and a translator is a fairly common site in Kyiv. But if there is a crowd it can get a little uncomfortable. This was perfect.

The weather was beautiful, so when we finished our meal, we decided to move out to the sidewalk café and have another glass of wine. Vlada was with us for about an hour when Oksana told her she wanted her to leave us alone. I paid Vlada, she confirmed her contact information, and she left.

From the time I met Oksana, there was no doubt that I wanted her luggage to go to my room. Nevertheless, I was prepared to get her a room, but it was never even mentioned. And now, she was sending me a clear message that she wanted to be alone with me.

After the first few days of messaging, our conversations had often wandered into the sensual area. Oksana was a very sexy woman, and she knew how to use that sexuality. Still, just because a woman liked to talk about being naked in the shower, it didn't mean she was ready for sex with someone she hadn't met. But it didn't feel like we had just met.

After Vlada left, we sat at our outside table for a while and talked. Oksana knew a little English, but we used Google translate most of the time. The electronic translation wasn't perfect and there were times when it was difficult and there were times when the translation was wrong. This was very important. It could cause some serious issues. On one occasion, Oksana was telling me about her nephew, and it was translated as her son. That's not even close.

We decided to go to the spa on the second floor of the hotel and get into the Jacuzzi. She wanted to get a massage, but she decided to wait until the next day for that. After the Jacuzzi, we went to the room.

There was no question about what was going to happen next. We were both hungry for sex and we had waited eight months. There was absolutely no hesitation and no reservation. We were having sex with each other for the first time, but it felt so natural that we were uninhibited and free. Oksana kissed me as I had never been kissed before. It was like she was extremely thirsty, and she was drinking water in large gulps. The sounds she made gave me the same sensation. It was as if she was trying to consume me. She was insatiable. She could not get enough, and neither could I.

We wanted to do everything that first time as if we wouldn't have another opportunity. It went on for hours. Sometime around midnight, we ordered a snack from room service. We ate the food and drank a glass of wine. When we got back in bed an hour later, the sex resumed where we left off. We finally fell asleep around 3:00 a.m.

The next morning, we got up around 11:00. I have never slept better. We both took showers. The word for shower in Russian is *douche*. This caused a little confusion at first. I thought Oksana was taking a lot of *douches*. She was only taking showers. It wasn't long before I was calling a shower, a *douche*.

Unbelievably, my first trip to Kyiv was for only five days. It makes no sense to plan a trip of 12,000 miles for five days. I still don't know why I did it. It's possible I might have been a little nervous about travel to Ukraine. Whatever the reason, it was a mistake.

Chapter Forty-Five

My first chore of the day was the unpleasant task of contacting Mila and telling her that there would be no reason for me to meet with her again. The only good news in this scenario was I didn't have to talk with her. I just sent her a Viber message. But the second I hit the send button; I had a bad feeling about it. I felt I was doing the right thing, but why did it feel so wrong? I think I mentioned that I am not the least bit superstitious.

After that ordeal, I returned my attention to Oksana. That was much easier to do. She was showered and dressed, and she was absolutely lovely.

We went downstairs to the little outside café and had breakfast. Breakfast is just another meal until there is someone special to share it with; it then becomes an event. If this is beginning to sound like love at first sight, I don't give a damn. It's my story and I'm going to tell it my way.

At breakfast, we planned our day. Oksana wanted to take a boat ride on the Dnieper River. So, she contacted a tour operator, and we grabbed a taxi to the docks. She was holding my hand in the cab, and I mentioned to her that her palm was wet. She told me it wasn't the only thing that was wet. Another Oscar nomination.

When we got to the river, we walked out to where our boat was docked. It was a nice boat. Oksana had made the arrangements and I had not asked her what it was going to cost. Since I'm a cautious guy, I thought

I might better determine the cost before the trip rather than after. When he quoted me 500 an hour, I thought he meant 500 hryvnias, or about $25 an hour. When the captain told me it was $500 an hour it made the decision incredibly easy. Oksana and I booked a river tour for the next day on another boat with about 50 other passengers. The total cost was about $50. We also hired a guide.

Since we skipped today's $500 boat ride, we quickly changed our plans to visit a large, beautiful park not far from the river. We took a cab there from the docks. The park was lovely. There are many great parks in Kyiv. The government doesn't mind spending money on buildings and parks. I guess the poor people would revolt if they weren't provided some places to enjoy that are almost free. They certainly can't afford anything else.

The best thing about the park was the live entertainment and the smell of meat cooking on the grill. We had a great time. The food was as good as it smelled. The live entertainment was good, and the park was crowded with families and lovers. It felt so good to be with Oksana. She smiled all of the time with that award-winning smile. And every fifteen minutes she said in perfect English, "Photo, please." I must have taken a thousand pictures of her during the next few months. Some of the photos were suitable for *Parents Magazine*. Some of the photos were more suitable for *Playboy*.

We spent the day at the park drinking beer and listening to music. Late in the day, we took a cab back to the Opera. We again took a *douche* and rested for an hour or so. The food was so good at Vino e Cucina that

I decided to take Oksana there. We got dressed and I asked the concierge to call for a taxi. Taxis were a bargain in Kyiv. You could go almost anywhere in the city for five dollars. The cab ride was ten minutes. We decided to sit inside because it was a little cool. The atmosphere was warm, and the wine and food were as good as I remembered. I didn't mention to Oksana that Mila and I had eaten there recently.

When the check came, it was delivered by the young lady who had been our waitress when Mila and I had eaten there a couple of nights before. It made me a little nervous, but she only wanted to tell me she greatly appreciated the twenty percent tip I had given her. The only problem was that she didn't get the tip. It seems the restaurants in Kyiv pocket the tips and give the staff little or nothing. This pissed me off. I gave the woman the tip that was taken from her and I never again added the tip to the check. From that time on, I paid the tip in cash directly to the staff.

The restaurant called a cab for us, and we returned to the hotel. We stopped by the bar at the hotel for a nightcap. I'm not much of a vodka drinker but you never say that in Russia. And, in my opinion, it's all Russia. (At the time I thought Putin and I agreed. That was before Putin turned into Stalin.) So, Oksana suggested we drink some vodka. The bartender poured some Grey Goose, and I took a sip. A sip isn't allowed in Russia, so I drank half of the vodka in one gulp. Half of the vodka in one gulp isn't allowed in Russia either. In fifteen minutes, I was drunk for the second time in ten years.

When Oksana and I got to the room and got into bed, the vodka we drank made little difference. We made love for hours. Yes, I know I changed from "had sex" to "made love" there. Again, it's my story.

During the four days Oksana and I were together in Kyiv we made love on seven different occasions. These were not quickies. They were marathon sessions, and they were wonderful. I couldn't recall anything like it in my life. Oksana had told me that sex was a very important thing in her life. She even told me the number one reason Ukrainian women leave their husbands is too little sex. I began to wonder how little sex was too little.

Oksana wanted me to buy her a laptop to help her communicate with me better. I was used to women asking me to buy them things, but this made sense to me. We contacted Vlada who agreed to meet us at a large shopping mall for lunch and computer shopping. We met at Ocean Plaza which is an ultra-modern shopping complex just a couple of kilometers from the hotel. It has all of the great shops from around the world, including a huge electronics store. Oksana picked out a laptop and a memory card. Then we ate lunch at a great sushi restaurant in the mall. Again, I was amazed at the quality of the food. Ukrainians take their food a lot more seriously than I had ever imagined.

The next two days in Kyiv were a blur. We walked around the city and saw the sights. We discovered little sidewalk cafés and we made love at the hotel. Late every afternoon we had a glass or two of the Ukrainian chardonnays at the hotel. It quickly became a tradition.

 The first time Oksana and I made love she had whispered "condom" in perfect English just before we began actual intercourse. Of course, I was prepared for this, and it was not an issue. However, on the night before I left Kyiv, I decided not to use protection. I hate the damn things. It interrupts the intimacy, and it is indeed like washing your feet with your socks on. When she insisted, I asked why? There are obvious reasons, of course, but I wanted to know if she was concerned about getting pregnant. She said she was. When I told her I had had a vasectomy she didn't understand. Even when we used the translator, she didn't know what I meant, so I googled the procedure, translated it, and handed her my iPad. When she read the definition, she immediately began to softly cry. At that moment I knew how important a baby was to her. She had told me she didn't have to have a baby in her life, but her biological clock was ticking loudly, and she was understandably wrestling with the issue.

It was an emotional night for both of us. I was thinking this might be the end of our relationship. I think she was dealing with the baby and some other complicated problems. We finally fell asleep around 4:00 a.m. We had about two hours to sleep before we had to get up and get ready to go to the airport.

When it came time for me to catch a cab to the airport, Oksana insisted she go with me. She didn't want to say goodbye at the hotel. The ride to the airport was sad. I didn't know when I would see her again. I knew I was falling in love. There was nothing I could do about it now.

When we got to the airport, I checked my bags, and we ate breakfast. After we had eaten, we sat at our table in the airport restaurant. Oksana had entered some text on her phone. She had translated it to English. The text reads, "We go to the men's restroom and have sex?" I thought she was kidding. She wasn't. I told her it was impossible. She was very disappointed, so I got up and checked out the men's restrooms. They are more open than in America and they were very busy. I reported this to her. She took me by the hand and led me to one of the restrooms. Men were going in and out. She said to me, "This is perfect." By this time, I was so excited I would have done just about anything. But I wouldn't go into a men's restroom at the airport in Kyiv for sex with anyone. And there was no one on the planet I would rather have sex with than Oksana.

The flight back to Amsterdam was depressing. Every minute I flew I was several miles farther away from Oksana. I was definitely in love.

Chapter Forty-Six

I was back in Birmingham on June 28, 2016. Oksana had finally given me her contact information in Kyiv and we were using Viber to communicate. This was so much easier than messaging through the site and it didn't cost anything. A simple copy and paste function is all that was needed for translation. After a short time, it became a very simple process.

But the mood of our correspondence had changed. I could tell Oksana was trying to slow down the process. At a time when I was certain of what I wanted, she was headed in the other direction. It could have been the baby. It could have been the age difference. It was likely both, along with some other issues that I would never completely understand.

When I read the transcript of our messaging around this time, it was obvious I was being too impatient, and she was not reacting to my impatience very well. She was asking for time, and I was asking for a decision.

On June 29, I wrote to her.

My Dearest Oksy,
I began this letter yesterday but I was too tired and my heart was too heavy to finish it. I slept well last night but my heart is still heavy. I know I told you I would give you some time to think about us. Well, I was wrong and I am sorry. You have all of the information you need to make a decision and I want you to make it.

I don't want you to worry about hurting me. Yes, it will hurt if you say no, but broken hearts mend.

I want you to know that I love you, but I can't live this far away from the woman I love and I can't just write letters for another nine months. So please tell me about us. I don't want to hear about your job or the weather in Ukraine. I just want to hear your decision about us.

All of my love.

Almost immediately, Oksana replied.

My Sweetheart,

I don't remember getting such a big letter from you. As you know, I am still tired from the trip. I can't make a decision this fast. You know how I plan everything. I need time to think about all of this, darling.

If you aren't prepared to wait for my decision, just tell me. You know I am not good at making fast decisions. And I must think of my children. My nephews and nieces mean everything to me. I don't know if I can leave them.

"Strangers in the Night" is playing on the radio again. Did you send it to me?

Oksana

Oksana suggested we stop communicating so much to give her time to think. In retrospect, it seems perfectly logical, but at the time, it was devastating to me. We had reached a stalemate. We stopped communicating for a few days. She sounded like her heart was broken. Mine certainly was.

On July 1, Oksana sent me a letter.

My Dear,

I slept almost none last night, dear. It is so hurtful for me. Now I sit at my job and realize the fairy tale is over. All was too good to be true. We waited too long for the meeting. The first meeting, I was alone. The second meeting was the most unbelievable thing of my life.
But you have made the right decision. Now you and I are both alone. I just can't stop these tears from falling from my eyes.
I will ask you if we can talk from time to time.
I just need time to think.
Thank you for understanding.
Oksana

I was hurting and I thought it had to end so I could move on with my life. I was convinced Oksana would never leave Ukraine and I couldn't see myself going to Ukraine every few months to visit. So I did one of the most difficult things I have ever done. I ended the relationship on July 7 with a short letter.

No, I am sorry Oksy, but we can't talk from time to time. I simply can't do that. I hope you find what you are looking for. I honestly hope you will be someone's woman for life.
Please don't contact me again.
I wish you only the best.

It sounds awful now. Hell, it was awful. But at the time, I didn't see another way out of a terrible situation. If I had been more patient, it might not have been so awful. I will never know for sure.

Chapter Forty-Seven

What I did next makes absolutely no sense to me now. Unfortunately, it made perfect sense to me then. I likely should have just given Oksana some time to sort things out. But I was desperate. All of the time and effort to find a long-term relationship had failed. I was depressed. I might have been heartbroken. I was certainly convinced that Oksana was not coming to the U.S.

I received a message from Mila almost immediately. She wanted to know how things had gone with my meeting with the other woman in Kyiv. I told her it had not gone well. To be honest, it had gone well—the results weren't what I wanted, but the meeting with Oksana was better than I could have hoped for.

When we first resumed our correspondence, Mila gave me the full "woman scorned" treatment. And she should have. I took it like a man, as they say. I had not treated her right, but she had reached back out to me, and that had helped my wounded feelings immensely. It wasn't long before we were right back where we were before the Kyiv fiasco.

Mila sent me some more of her professional pictures. These just confirmed what I already knew. Her appearance had not been the problem. Her apparent coldness had been the problem. She must have sensed this because she began sending me warm and intimate messages on Viber. She told me she liked me a lot and wanted me to consider a long-term relationship with her. It was all so fast and so different. I was surprised at the change in her attitude. I began to think this might work.

A few days later, Mila sent me a picture of an engagement ring. It was a beautiful ring. The diamond was about the right size. She told me she had been out shopping with a friend and they had wandered into a jewelry store. The story sounded plausible, but the implication was undeniable. A woman would never send this message unless she had a reason to send it. I was shocked at the suggestion, so I asked her if she was getting married any time soon. She told me she was looking just in case I wanted to buy her a ring. She said she just wanted to be ready.

Ukraine Brides warns men not to purchase expensive gifts for the ladies. They specifically mention expensive engagement rings. The potential scam is simple. The woman takes the man to a jewelry store where she has been looking at rings. She picks out a few for him to look at. They agree on a ring, and he makes the purchase. When the man leaves Ukraine, the woman returns the ring to the jeweler and gets most of the money refunded. The jeweler keeps a portion for his trouble.

So, there were two likely scenarios. Either Mila was honestly interested in me for possible marriage, or she was trying to earn some quick money. I didn't tell Mila but there was no way I was going to leave an expensive ring and a woman in Ukraine when I returned to Birmingham.

Mila wanted me to come back to Ukraine and meet with her. She said she had been missing me since I left. Her messages bordered on suggestive and were different from the woman I had met in Kyiv. I was very close to telling her I just couldn't come back to Ukraine so soon. Then I looked at all of her pictures, I recalled how lovely she was, I considered her changed attitude, and I did something that was even more ridiculous than my first trip to Ukraine. I booked my second trip to Kyiv.

I had been home for only three weeks, and I was on an airplane to Kyiv. This time I was forced to fly through Paris. I love Paris, but as I mentioned, I don't like the airport. It's not the language—I know a little French. It's the signage throughout the airport. They would have to try hard to make it any worse. The consolation was the flight from Atlanta to Paris was on Air France. I don't think I have ever been on an Air France flight where you couldn't get more wine by simply asking. The French can fuck up a two-car funeral, but they have wine nailed.

Mila wanted to rent a car for my week in Kyiv. She liked to drive, and she wanted to take me on some short driving tours. I thought this was a great idea, so I told her to arrange for a vehicle. When I arrived at Boryspil International in Kyiv, Mila was waiting. Her smiling face was a beautiful sight after the long flight and the border ordeal. She seemed so happy to see me. Maybe she did like me after all.

We walked the short distance to the parking lot. As we were pulling out of the lot, I exhaled and thanked her for the invitation and for picking me up at the airport. She was wearing some fashionable jeans that were totally worn out and totally in style all over the world. I think they are advertised as "destroyed." I am serious.

There was a hole in her jeans in the thigh area. I patted her leg and told her it was good to see her again. She looked at my hand like it was a tarantula. I knew I had done the wrong thing, but I didn't know exactly what that thing was. I now think it would have been fine to rub her leg, but the pat somehow resembled a hit and Ukrainian women can't stand that. It might have something to do with the fact that they are often abused by men. But I don't know.

Eventually, Mila told me she didn't like what I did in the car as we left the airport. I told her I was happy she had brought it up because I had no idea what I did. She told me a gentle stroke is acceptable but a pat or a hit is not. I told her it was a show of affection in America. We often pat people on the back for a job well done and to show someone we care about them. She told me none of that was acceptable in Ukraine. Well, you learn something new every day. Unfortunately, the habit was ingrained, and I would make the same mistake in the future with her and others.

Mila got over the incident quickly and we had a pleasant enough drive to the hotel. I checked in and went to my room with the bellman. Mila waited for me in the lobby. It was late in the afternoon, and I was tired from the trip, but we had a glass of wine in the lobby and chatted. Mila was hungry so we decided to walk to a little café just up the street from the hotel. There were several great places to eat within easy walking distance of the hotel. The restaurant Mila chose was not one of them.

We ate something forgettable, and Mila asked me if I wanted to smoke a hookah pipe. I had never heard of a hookah pipe. The first thing I thought was she was going to smoke some kind of drug that must be legal in Ukraine. I don't smoke anything, so I wasn't interested. Mila ordered a pipe, and one was quickly delivered to our table. I didn't fully understand how the thing worked but it must have had a heating element in it that created steam that was drawn through flavored tobacco, then through a hose and into your lungs. It smelled better than it sounds. I took a couple of gulps just to be sociable. Though it did nothing for me, it must do something for the young people of Ukraine because we later saw them in almost every bar we visited.

It was early, but I was tired and needed to get horizontal. We walked back to the Opera Hotel. Mila and I chatted for a little while outside the hotel. We decided when we would meet in the morning. Then she said goodnight, got into the rental car, and went home.

Despite my travel fatigue, I was surprised that there was almost no show of intimacy or affection. I am never too tired to hug, kiss, and make love to a woman, but I could tell that was not in the cards tonight. I would soon discover the card wasn't even in the deck.

I considered this somewhat sexually suggestive Now back to my story.

Chapter Forty-Eight

The next morning Mila drove to the Opera Hotel and met me for breakfast. We ordered some toast and coffee at the sidewalk café. It was another gorgeous day, and the food and coffee were wonderful. Mila wore a white dress with some kind of small red pattern. She was lovely. Every time I saw her I couldn't get over her beauty. Some of it is the way Ukrainian women take care of themselves. But, in Mila's case, it was mostly her natural beauty. I very often thought what a shame all of that natural beauty and sexiness was wasted on such a cold and unaffectionate woman.

Mila wanted to take me to Mariyinsky Park. The park is more than 130 years old. There are several large government buildings nearby. There are elaborate fountains and sculptures of famous Ukrainian and Russian men and women—I didn't recognize any of the names, but Mila told me they were famous.

The temperature was very pleasant for July. There was a gentle breeze that moved Mila's dress in just the right way. We had gotten coffee and had sat down on a park bench to relax and drink. I found it very difficult to keep my hands off her. It seemed perfectly natural to reach out and touch her or hold her hand, but I was afraid I was going to run her away. So, I did nothing.

We spent most of the day at the park. I took some pictures of Mila. She seemed very happy. We sat down on a ledge that encircled a fountain and watched the people walk by. I decided to use my shock factor. I asked, "Mila, how do you feel about sex?"

She said, "I love sex." I asked her how people go from not touching to having sex. She said, "They get married."

I had forgotten there were people in the world who believed that sex is only appropriate after marriage. I don't think there is any way I would ever marry a woman with whom I had not had sex. From a practical standpoint, I want to make sure she has all of the equipment. I also want to make certain we are sexually compatible. As incredible as it may sound, I began to wonder if Mila was frigid or if she might be a man who was made up to look like a woman. In my opinion, there was something very wrong with this picture.

Mila drove us back to the hotel. She told me she needed to go home and freshen up for dinner and that she would be back to pick me up in two hours. I went to my room alone. I took a shower and went down to the lobby for a glass of my favorite local chardonnay and waited for Mila. She came walking through the front doors of the hotel looking like a model. Again, I thought, what a waste.

We went to a place in the middle of town where young people go. I think the area was called Arena City. There was music, bars, restaurants, and a lot of people. We walked around for a while just looking at the beautiful people. We decided to go to a bar that was located upstairs over a gentlemen's club. The place was packed but most of the people were standing, so we were able to get a table quickly. When we were seated, Mila ordered a hookah pipe, and I ordered a shot of Patrón tequila. Someone immediately set up the hookah pipe. Several people were doing the hookah thing and I was getting used to it.

I ordered a double Patrón. I was not happy. Mila had enticed me to Ukraine, suggesting she liked me and was interested in a long-term relationship. I just happen to think a long-distance relationship begins with a single step. Yes, I know I am combining metaphors here, but you get the idea. How can you get to third base if you don't go by first and second? Mila and I weren't even in the same ballpark.

So, the tequila and I asked Mila what she had in mind regarding our relationship. She told Patrón and me that she wanted to get married. She was looking for a soulmate. She wanted to find a man she could spend the rest of her life with. I couldn't help but wonder when the rest of her life would begin. I also wondered, why not tonight?

Mila wanted to stay out late. I wanted to go to the hotel and get in bed with her. But I never said that. This woman was driving me crazy. I wasn't thinking clearly. It wasn't just the tequila. It was the 6,000 miles, the sensuous messages, the provocative dress, the beautiful body, her sexy behavior, and her coldness that were killing me. I didn't know what to do. But I knew I wasn't going to wait until we were married to find out if there was a penis under that dress.

Okay, I said it. I apologize. Now, what was I going to do about it? As Mila drove us back to the hotel, I decided that I would ask her to come inside and have a drink with me at the hotel bar. I wasn't going to ask her to come to my room for hot sex. I was trying to find a way to determine if we had a scintilla of potential. I was flying by the seat of my pants. That was what I always did. That was the reason I was in Kyiv.

When we pulled up in front of the Opera Hotel, I asked Mila if she wanted to come inside for a nightcap. She told me she had some legal work to do tomorrow and needed to get to bed. I felt this was a little inconsistent with her desire to stay out late at Arena City, so I took out my wallet and gave her the money for the rental car and told her goodnight. I didn't try to kiss her.

When I got out of bed the next morning, there were several Viber messages on my cellphone. Mila had our day planned. It would have been easy to ask her to pick me up in an hour. What I did was send her this Viber message, "Mila, I have tried my best to do what you have asked me to do. I hope you find someone who can keep their hands off you until you are happily married. I am not that man. I am sorry. I wish you the best." You might get away with dumping a woman once, but that second time is virtually always the coup de gras.

Later I learned that Mila had gotten married. I'm not surprised. I was likely wrong about her. I believe she will be a wonderful wife. It would have helped if she had talked with me about her firm beliefs. If I only had a brain….

Chapter Forty-Nine

Earlier I mentioned parts of this true story might be unbelievable. This is another one of those parts. They are adding up.

Before returning to Kyiv, I had registered on another website for Ukrainian women called Victoria Brides. I chatted with several young women on the site. They were the usual beautiful Ukrainian women. They were clearly on the same program as the women on Ukraine Brides. They enticed men to message them for a price, and then they split the fee with the website. When gifts were delivered, the website charged two prices and split the revenue with the lady. This was a very simple business. It is a Ukrainian industry. Welcome to Ukraine.

One night while browsing the site I stumbled across a woman I recognized immediately. It was Oksana. It was like an electric shock when I saw her picture. She had even made a video. I clicked on it. Oksana said in near-perfect English, "Hello, my name is Oksana. I am from the city of Kharkiv. I am on Victoria Brides looking for a husband for my life." I couldn't believe it. Here was the woman I had fallen in love with advertising herself to the world a few days after I had spent four days in bed with her in Kyiv. Of course, here I was as well.

Most people would have turned off the computer, had a stiff drink, and gone to bed. They would have never gone on that website again. But I am not most people. I sent her a message on the site. You can imagine the tone of my message. She replied that I had left her, and she was trying to move on with her life.

Oksana and I communicated for a couple of days. I told her for the first time about my first meeting in Kyiv with Mila. I told her that Mila was a backup for her in case she didn't show. I told her the truth. I told her when I met her the following day, I had ended my relationship with Mila. I also told her I was now planning a trip back to Kyiv to try to salvage my relationship with Mila. She appeared upset and shocked to hear that I was returning to Ukraine so quickly. But surprisingly, she told me to let her know if I wanted to see her while I was in Kyiv. How could this possibly get more bizarre?

When I ended the relationship with Mila, the first thing I thought about was sending a message to Oksana. I didn't think there was a chance in Hell she would come to Kyiv, but she had asked me to let her know if I had time for her. Well, I certainly had five days to kill in the city and the thought of spending them alone was unimaginable, so I sent a message to Oksana and asked her to come to Kyiv. She replied that she would be on the train the following day. I was fucking blown away.

Chapter Fifty

Every time I met Oksana in Kyiv it was exciting. At least we were now communicating by Viber, and I could keep up with where she was located. The train from Kharkiv to Kyiv runs in and out of areas with Wi-Fi, so the connection is sporadic, but I at least knew she was on the train I would know if there was a delay or some other issues.

Oksana sent me a message when she arrived at the train station. I couldn't wait to see her, but I wondered how it would go considering all we had been through during the past few weeks. It was wonderful seeing her walk into the Opera Hotel. She had that perfect smile on her face, and she had cut her hair. I should not have worried. We started where we left off. We didn't skip a beat. We didn't talk about Mila.

It was early evening when Oksana arrived at the hotel. We went directly to the room. We decided to order some food from room service. She ordered a large Caesar salad, and I chose the cold meat platter. We decided to share our dishes. The food was outstanding. We had ordered a bottle of the good chardonnay. We were both hungry. It was a feast.

We talked for an hour or so and then got into bed. Oksana gave great massages and she had brought some oil for the purpose. I used my cellphone to take several pictures of us while she was giving me the massage. Looking at those pictures is still difficult. I have taken them off my phone, but they are still on my laptop. I just can't seem to be able to hit the delete button.

One reason they are still difficult to view is that the lovemaking after the massage was so good. We hadn't seen each other for nearly a month, and we were making up. That was a great combination for sex. Oksana was insatiable. Her kisses were the familiar aggressive water gulping that always drove me crazy. Now she had added some biting to her routine. These were bites that hurt a little. She bit my tongue, my neck, and my shoulders. The bites left marks. That had never happened to me before. She was very sexually aroused but she was also punishing me for what I had done to her.

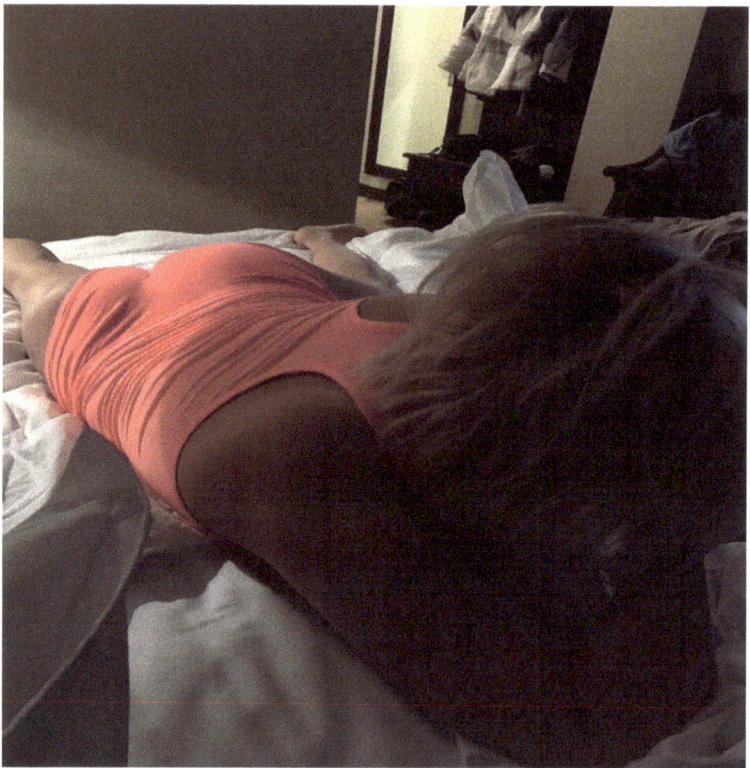

Oksana in our room at the Opera Hotel

Oksana gives what would be considered a sports massage. It is a little rough for my taste, but not much. The massage she gave me that first night was even rougher than usual. I think she was trying to hurt me. I completely understood.

Oksana is a short muscular woman. She is about five feet tall and weighs about 110 pounds. She was a gymnast in college, and she works out several times a week. No doubt, pound for pound, she is the strongest woman I have ever been with. One night while we were in bed, we had a little argument. The next thing I know, I am on the floor. She had thrown me out of the bed. I am an average-sized man. I am five feet ten inches tall, and I weigh about 170 pounds. She had taken me by surprise. When I got back in bed, I was going to return the favor and throw her out of the bed. She was prepared for my move, and we wrestled for a while. The match got a little rough and somehow my elbow hit her in the mouth. There was some blood on her teeth. I felt awful. I apologized profusely. I was so embarrassed and angry with myself. She went into the bathroom to clean up. When she came back, I continued to apologize. We were playing but there is never a reason for a man to hit a woman.

Oksana got back into the bed and acted as if nothing had happened. She had started the fight, and all was fair in love and war. She told me she knew it was an accident and she never mentioned it again.

I have often wondered how a man would fair in a fight to the finish with various animals. For example, I believe a man in good physical condition would stand a pretty good chance in a fight with a small bobcat. I think he would have at least an even chance of surviving. If he did survive, he would be a bloody pulp, but he would be alive. That's about the way I felt about a serious fight with Oksana. I knew my size and strength would prevail, but she would do some serious damage in the process. She was a strong little woman.

Chapter Fifty-One

The following four days in Kyiv were about as good as it got. We settled into our routine of morning coffee and a light breakfast at the sidewalk café and a glass or two of chardonnay in the lobby in the evening. Then, sandwiched in between, were little excursions just to make things more interesting.

The Lobby of the Opera Hotel in Kyiv

We began to visit some eating places within walking distance of the hotel. One of these was a restaurant called Piccolino on Oleisa Honchara Street just down the hill for the Opera Hotel. It was owned by laFamiliglia. This is the same company that owned Vino e Cucina.

Piccolino was a world-class northern Italian-style restaurant. I have been to more than twenty–five countries and I have eaten at some great restaurants, and the food and atmosphere here compared favorably with the very best. On one trip to Piccolino, I took a picture of a quail dinner I had ordered. Several months later Google sent me a notification that more than 5,000 people had viewed the picture. A lot of people liked this place. These people had good taste.

During one of our meals at Piccolino, I asked Oksana if she was going to America. She whispered, "Yes."

I said, "Oksy, what did you just say?"

She raised her hands in the air and shouted, "Yes, I am going to America!" I have had some happy moments in my life but this one was right up there near the top. I took a picture of her with her hands up in the air. It was a reenactment, but I don't think I will ever be able to delete that picture from my computer. She was wearing a black dress. She was beautiful, and she had agreed to come to America.

Piccolino was special, but just a block down the street was a little place called Café Room 88. The food there was inexpensive and consistently good. Two people could have lunch there for less than ten dollars. We had become regulars; they knew who we were, and they smiled when we walked in.

On one visit to Café Room 88, I ordered a salad topped with mandarin chicken. It was a delicious meal I ordered often, but today the salad came with something extra. As I was picking up a bite with my fork, I noticed a small wire staple in the lettuce. It was difficult to see, and I was fortunate to have noticed it. It might not have caused serious harm, but I didn't want to risk it. These things happen when humans are involved and the last thing, I wanted to do was cause a scene in the restaurant, so I picked out the staple, secretly placed it under the edge of my plate, and continued to eat my meal. But it wasn't a secret to Oksana. She immediately asked me what was wrong. I told her nothing was wrong. She said, "I saw you put something under your plate."

I replied, "Oksy, don't worry about it. It was just a small wire staple that likely held the lettuce together during shipping."

She looked at it and said, "Oh my god!" She called the waitress over to the table, and just as I expected, there was a crisis to deal with. I was saying everything was okay and Oksana was talking loudly in Russian. It sounded like she was saying everything wasn't okay.

Ukrainian people are demonstrative. They will appear to yell at each other and then smile and say the Russian word for thank you. It's pronounced spah-see-boh. I learned the word very early because, thank you, works wonders in any language. This, however, was different. Oksana was upset about the foreign material in my salad, and she was letting them know it. You would have thought I had found a dead mouse in my food. The chef came out to our table and apologized. When things finally settled down, we finished our meal and I asked for the check. When we were told there would be no charge for the meal Oksana was happy, but I was having none of this; I finally put my foot down.

In Ukraine, the man was the boss. There could be disagreement, and there often was, but when it came down to the final decision, it was the man who made the call. So, I made the call and Oksana backed down.

When the waitress brought my receipt there was a small bag of goodies for us to take with us to the hotel. It was a peace offering for a war that should never have happened. This was the second time I saw Oksana's temper and it was not a pretty sight.

Chapter Fifty-Two

Kyiv is a beautiful old city. The Russian influence is everywhere. Ukraine was a part of Russia until 1991.

The Ukraine Revolution of 2014 took place not far from the Opera Hotel. A series of violent events, involving protestors, riot police, and unknown shooters, resulted in the deaths of 113 people. More than 1,800 people were wounded; some of the wounded were minors. According to a well-known Ukrainian doctor, the "snipers were aiming at the heart, lungs, and necks" of the protestors.

Oksana and I spent a lot of time walking around the city during each of our visits here. On one particularly gorgeous day, we were looking at some artwork along a sidewalk when I noticed what appeared to be some bullet holes in the walls of the buildings. Next to some of the holes were names and dates. Oksana told me this was where most of the young protestors were killed in 2014. The names on the walls were memorials to those people. It seemed incredible to me that this could have happened only two years before our casual stroll among the lovely original artwork. It reminded me of how precarious life could be even in a large cosmopolitan city like Kyiv.

The United States Department of State recommended visitors to Kyiv register with the U.S. Embassy there. They want a lot of information including where you are staying while in the city and your contact information. I always registered. I never knew exactly why they made this request for information. When my friends asked me why they wanted to know where I was staying, I told them they likely just wanted to know where to come to get the body. They failed to see the humor in this. I thought it was funny, but my mind wasn't firing on all cylinders at the time—and it's not a high-performance engine anyway.

Chapter Fifty-Three

Strolling along the streets of Kyiv was such a pleasant thing to do. There were no significant day-to-day responsibilities and Oksana, and I were always holding hands. It was on the regular walks that I first became aware of just how superstitious Oksana was. At first, I thought she was just having a little harmless fun with me. She knew I had been hesitant about coming to Ukraine because of the small issue of the Russians killing people there. So, I thought she was just playing with me.

As in most large cities in the world, Kyiv has a huge parking problem. People park everywhere. The sidewalk is one of their favorite places. So, the city puts metal posts in the middle of some of the sidewalks to discourage this practice. They are about three feet tall, and they are everywhere.

When Oksana and I were walking around the city, we would often encounter these metal posts. When she insisted we pass on the same side of the post, I thought she was kidding. Of course, I understood the symbolism of something "coming between us," but I didn't think she was serious about it. She wasn't just serious about it; she was religious about it.

It would have been very convenient for us to just raise our coupled hands a few inches and avoid the posts, but that would not have avoided letting the obstacle come between us. So, on the very busy sidewalks of this city, we had to maneuver around every single one of them. This rule also applied to trees and other objects both inside and out.

I later learned that superstition was rampant in Ukraine. I didn't believe in the supernatural and I found this incredible. Almost everyone in the world thinks differing beliefs is nonsense. Believing what they believe, however, makes perfect sense. And being superstitious made perfect sense to Oksana.

Oksana has a friend in her city of Kharkiv who advised her on spiritual matters. When she first told me about it I immediately thought of the fortunetellers I use to see occasionally along the side of the road—I don't see them very often anymore but I am sure they are still there. Oksana would often call her friend to seek her advice. If she had a difficult decision to make, she would call Tanya. If she was having a bad day and needed some spiritual guidance to get her out of her funk, she would call Tanya. I never asked her what she paid the woman, but I am certain her magic services weren't free.

I referred to Tanya as Oksana's witch. I thought this was funny but that was before I began to understand how serious Oksana was about Tanya's advice. I quit calling Tanya her witch because I saw how critically important the spiritual advice had become. No matter where Oksana and I were, she was always mysteriously connected to Tanya by some magic communication system in the ether. It was mindboggling to me, but so was religion. What did I know?

Chapter Fifty-Four

I quickly got used to avoiding obstacles that threatened to split us asunder. I even tried not to make a big deal about it while thinking it was bullshit. I had a little more trouble getting used to some of the other Ukrainian customs.

I know it is a familiar custom in a lot of societies for everyone to remove their shoes when they come inside. I completely understand the concept. I was raised on a farm, and I am well aware of the potentially unpleasant results if you walk inside from the cow pasture. Checking the soles of your shoes is a common and necessary practice. And I understand the theory of keeping the inside of the house clean. But I don't understand removing your shoes every single time you come into a hotel room. The only explanation is that it is a custom.

In most indoor entrances in Ukraine, there is a shoe rack provided for the purpose. If there isn't a shoe rack, you simply place your shoes neatly by the door. There are no exceptions. If, for example, you need to go to the toilet and you have barely made it to the room, you must first remove your shoes.

I wanted to honor Oksana's customs because I knew they were important to her. I knew this would tell her how much I loved and respected her. But, when she began to yell at me with the usual "Take your shoes off!", I quickly became annoyed and frustrated. I think if she had been a little more patient and had asked me to take my shoes off it would not have become such a big issue.

Chapter Fifty-Five

Another custom in Ukraine, and all of Eastern Europe, is the code of chivalry. Women in Ukraine want the man to be the head of the family. They expect the man to make the final decisions about virtually everything. In return, the man is expected to treat the woman like a lady. I am pretty good at this because I was raised in the south of U.S. and I was taught from a very early age how to treat a lady. But customs have changed in my country during my lifetime and men are often confused about what women want.

I was talking with a bright Ukrainian woman recently and she told me the reason American men are so attracted to Russian women—she considers all Ukrainian women to be Russian. She told me women all over the world had some fundamental female urges they couldn't control. These urges were complicated and tied to women's biological makeup and evolution. A woman wanted her man to protect and provide for her and her offspring. She wanted him to be strong and capable of defending her against others who might hurt her or her offspring in any way. Of course, there were other needs, but these were the most fundamental of all.

This Ukrainian woman, who had a very successful business putting Russian women and American men together, further explained to me the problem with American women. She told me American women were confused about what they wanted in a man.

They, like all women in the world, had the same biological needs. However, they were now conflicted by issues like equal pay and women's rights. They were torn between often conflicting goals. The result of this was that men were also confused about what to offer American women.

I know this is a controversial and complicated issue, but this woman has built her very successful business based almost exclusively on this philosophy.

So, contrary to popular opinion, men were interested in foreign women because most of these women had traditional relationship values. They were ready to fulfill the traditional expectations of a woman and they expected the same from their man. If a man appeared weak and indecisive, she would not be interested in him at all. And even though a lot of foreign women had become somewhat "westernized," that had been my observation in Ukraine.

Oksana was married for a few years, but she had spent most of her adult life working. This exposure had slightly affected her traditional view of the relationship between a man and a woman. But she held onto the fundamental Ukrainian values. Later, when I met her mother and father, it was very obvious that these values had been handed down from them. And her parents were not confused at all about the matter.

Oksana fully expected me to open doors for her. She expected me to pull her chair out for her at the dining table. She waited for me to help her remove her coat and shoes when we entered the hotel room. It took a little while for me to get used to it. At first, she might be standing there waiting for me to open the cab door. But it didn't take me long to be there for her every time.

She almost demanded chivalry because of her traditional values. I was happy to oblige. But I must confess I had gotten accustomed to women in America who sometimes wanted to do things for themselves. And it's this "sometimes" that confuses the hell out of some of us men. But that is just my opinion.

I want to add there is something sexual about helping a woman out of her coat and shoes. You are removing a garment and when you are removing her shoes it is an opportunity to give her feet a quick little massage. No wonder these customs became such a tradition. I completely understand most of them.

Chapter Fifty-Six

On one of our walking tours, Oksana and I visited Saint Sophia's Cathedral again. The church was located on Volodymyrska Street. There were always a lot of street vendors in the area selling cheap souvenirs. Today there was also a woman with some trained pigeons. At first, I thought she was feeding the pigeons in the area. But she had brought her birds to the marketplace. She was trying to charge tourists for taking a picture while they were holding her birds. I am not crazy about birds sitting on my shoulder for obvious reasons, but she could see we were tourists, and she began putting several of the pigeons on our shoulders. Of course, Oksana began saying her usual, "photo please, photo please" and the woman had us hooked.

After the woman took a couple of pictures with my cellphone, I was done with the pigeons, and I handed them back to her. She then wanted to charge us a ridiculous price for taking the pictures. Oksana gave her a piece of her mind and a dollar or two and we left. I still have those pictures on my laptop. They will be very difficult to delete.

After we left the bird-woman, we crossed the street and made another quick pass by Saint Michaels Golden-Domed Monastery. Saint Michael is Kyiv's patron saint. I have no idea what that means, though. This building was built in 2001. It replaced the original which was built in 1108 and torn down by the Soviets in 1937. It was spectacular, but what a colossal waste of money. That is just my humble opinion.

On the way back to the Opera Hotel we stopped by a beer garden and had lunch. There was a crowd there, so we assumed the food was good. We were not disappointed. The food was tasty, and the Ukrainian beer was superb. I ordered a regular size, and it was huge. I don't think beer comes in the small size in Ukraine.

After we finished lunch, we walked for twenty minutes and were back at the hotel. Oksana had an appointment for a massage in the hotel spa and I wanted to work out in the gym. I tried the sauna, but I have never understood how that much heat could be good for anything except roasting.

After ten minutes, I had had enough. We went to the Jacuzzi and relaxed for an hour. There was no one in the huge Jacuzzi except the two of us. Oksana wanted to give me a blowjob. I didn't want to disappoint her, so I consented. Of course, she wanted pictures of the act and I couldn't refuse that either. I also took several pictures of her in some seductive poses. She told me to send all of the photos to her on Viber, as usual.

Chapter Fifty-Seven

One thing Oksana and I did in Kyiv that was very interesting to me was grocery shop. I know that sounds weird, but I enjoyed putting together a little menu, picking up the supplies, and preparing a small meal in the hotel room. I was used to cooking for myself and I wanted to prepare some simple dishes for Oksana. We didn't cook anything in the room, but we did put together some tasty dishes. We would also pick up a couple of bottles of good wine or champagne to put in the refrigerator in the room. It was a lot less expensive than the hotel prices and it was better wine than in the little half bottles in the room mini bar.

One dish Oksana loved was my tomato mozzarella salad. It was very simple and simply delicious. It was a combination of nice, ripe tomatoes, fresh basil, buffalo mozzarella cheese, virgin olive oil, good balsamic vinegar, salt and pepper. If the ingredients were good, the results could be magical. I tried not to eat a lot of carbohydrates, but Oksana insisted on a French baguette to go with the salad. The combination was delicious. We always dipped the bread in the olive oil and balsamic vinegar in the salad. With a good French white, burgundy, it was hard to beat.

I also prepared a smoked salmon appetizer that was easy and delightful. It was just smoked salmon, cream cheese, sour cream, olive oil, fresh dill weed, lemon juice, salt, pepper, and some capers on a thin slice of the French baguette. Oksana thought I was a world-class chef. She often called me "chef." I guess Ukrainian men don't usually do a "woman's job."

The winter view from our room at the Opera Hotel

Another reason I liked grocery shopping was you could get to know a lot about people in their country by watching them shop. The grocery store where we shopped was located about four blocks from the hotel. In all kinds of weather, we would go to that store about every other day and haul supplies back to our room. If we needed anything else, we called room service, and they brought it immediately. We even asked for salt and pepper one night. Ten minutes later it was delivered to the door. I guess when you are a guest at the hotel for 60 days in one year you get special treatment. Something told me they treated every guest pretty special.

Chapter Fifty-Eight

Oksana often said our times together at the Opera Hotel were like a honeymoon. They weren't real life. She was right. There was no pressure. We got out of bed when we liked, we ate and drank what we wanted, and someone else cleaned up after us. When you are living the good life with a beautiful woman at your side, time flies. But it was soon the night before my return flight home.

We knew it would be some time before we saw each other again. As it turned out, it would be two and a half months. We held each other most of the night. We made love several times because we knew it would be a long time before we would be able to do it again. Absence does make the heart grow fonder and the anticipation of absence can have the same effect.

Small cultural differences can have a huge impact on a relationship too. Oksana always made sure she took me to the airport. She would ride in the cab with me and wait at the airport until I cleared customs. Technically, she saw me out of her country. Only then would she go to the train station for her trip back home. Much later, if I had remembered the importance of this custom, it might have made a difference in the outcome of our relationship. I don't think it would have made a difference, but it is possible.

Saying goodbye at the airport was one of the most difficult things about our long-distance affair. It's like you have no control of the situation. The plans are made in advance, and they are very difficult to change, so you just follow the itinerary despite the usual unfortunate consequences.

Every time my flight left, there was this deep feeling of loss. I knew how fast the plane was flying and I couldn't stop my brain from calculating the miles. Eventually, when I arrived in Birmingham, the clicker would read 6,000. My body would be home, but my heart would still be in Ukraine.

Chapter Fifty-Nine

Distrust and suspicion are the partners that can destroy a relationship. If your lover is located across town, it is easy to feel secure. If he or she is on the other side of the planet, all kinds of thoughts begin to enter your mind.

I felt certain that Oksana had not been truthful with me about several issues. She had an accounting degree, but she never once mentioned an accounting issue. She worked at a bank, but she could travel often with little notice to the bank. She had confused my name on at least three occasions, but she had a quick answer for each of these. When you desperately want something to succeed, you lose objectivity. That's just another way of saying love is blind.

Most couples who are seriously involved in a long-distance relationship are on video chats virtually every day. Skype is a very popular website but there are many others. The video calls are free. I don't understand how this pays the bills, but it has vastly improved worldwide communication and kept people closer than ever. The pain of separation is lessened greatly by these video calls. It hasn't been that long since we were sending cables overseas. Then, we were paying for expensive telephone calls. Now, we pay nothing for a video call. I think it is incredible.

I also thought it was incredible that Oksana seldom found time to talk to me on a video call. She said she loved me, but was satisfied to send emails and Viber chats. I have already mentioned that I never once initiated a video call with her. She insisted that she make the calls. And the calls were few and far between. There was a reason for her not wanting to receive video calls from me and that reason began to create distrust and suspicion in our relationship.

During the following few weeks, some additional suspicious activities caused me to question Oksana's honesty. A few of her Viber texts didn't exactly fit the conversation, and she got my name wrong again. Translations can be dead wrong and that must be taken into consideration. But the mistakes she was making were piling up and they eventually became impossible for me to ignore.

One of my good friends has a friend who married a woman from Kharkiv, the same city where Oksana lives. I had talked with him on the telephone about travel to Ukraine. He had given me some very helpful information about a lot of issues and answered my travel questions. We talked often and even tried to co-ordinate a trip together, but it never materialized.

It was in late August that I mentioned to Charles that I was having some doubts about some of the things Oksana was telling me. I told him I was having a difficult time handling my doubts. He told me he had a good friend in Kharkiv who could get anything done. Vitaly was a concierge at one of the leading hotels in Kharkiv. I knew from experience that a concierge in Ukraine could, indeed, deliver the goods. So, I asked Charles to contact Vitaly and see if he could gather some information about Oksana.

My friends told me if I was having doubts about Oksana's honesty, I should just end the relationship. That would have been easy if I hadn't been in love with her. But I was in love with her and I wanted to do everything possible to make it work.

The day after I talked with Charles, he called me and told me Vitaly could find out anything I wanted to know about Oksana. He said Vitaly was waiting for me to contact him directly. He gave me Vitaly's Viber contact information and I sent him a message. There is an eight-hour time difference between Birmingham and Kharkiv and it was the following day before I heard from Vitaly. He was very friendly and offered to help me in any way he could. That is the job description of a Ukrainian concierge. Welcome to Ukraine.

I told him about my issues with Oksana. He asked me to give him a day or two to make contact with someone who was an expert in the information-gathering business. Later in the same day, I received a message from Vitaly that he had contacted a friend who worked with the Ukraine Secret Service but who also did private investigative work on the side. I was not feeling good about this whole investigation idea and the mention of a Ukrainian policeman made me feel even worse. I considered dropping the entire idea, but I needed the information if I was going to continue to spend the time, money, and emotional capital on a Ukrainian woman with some very strange habits. So, I asked Vitaly to get me a price quotation for the investigation.

The next day Vitaly messaged me and told me it would cost $200 to gather the public and private information on Oksana. I was certain this was a simple computer search, but the price sounded reasonable to me. He said if I wanted to follow her, the cost would be an additional $100 a day. His friend estimated it would take four or five days to do the work and write a report. The very idea of this covert investigation made me physically sick, but I felt like I had to know, so I told him to go ahead with the project.

The following day, Vitaly sent me a Viber message and a written report on Oksana. The report gave her passport number, her employment registration number, and her address. The report further stated that she did not work at a bank. It said she had worked at a power company until 2005. Shockingly, the report stated she was married. There was some additional detailed information in the report about her husband.

Of course, I was devastated. This explained her secretiveness. However, three days later Vitaly contacted me again and changed the report. He had been mistaken about her being married. Oksana was officially divorced, as she had told me. She had no children and she had worked at the bank until June 30, 2015. Since that time, she had been unemployed.

So, she had lied about her being presently employed by the bank, but most everything else appeared to be true. A few days later I told Vitaly that Oksana had gone to the gym to work out that evening. His friend reported that there was no gym in the area. The nearest gym was a long way from where Oksana lived and the area is so dangerous that not even a man would be walking there at night. Vitaly said, "There are many bad guys in that area." The next day he sent me a written report that was very disturbing.

Vitaly's report stated, "I have some emergency information for you today. Friday and Saturday Oksana was talking with a woman friend. Nothing special happened. She was out of her flat two times. Nothing was unusual. Sunday, they didn't watch her. Today they started early in the morning, and they didn't see her for a long time. Then they decided to use other methods. They checked her location on her cellphone. They began to follow her to a different place. There she met a man who is an ex-policeman.

She spent a lot of time with him. We suspect that she lives with this man. I have attached photos of the meeting. She is certainly not working anywhere. To have undeniable proof they will need an additional two or three days of surveillance. One of the investigators was within one meter of her. He reported that she had many conversations with different men on her cellphone."

Two days later Vitaly delivered the crushing blow. His report simply said, "Now there is no doubt Oksana is a prostitute. The investigators didn't follow her today. They simply called her and met with her. She proposed her 'services' and showed some photos from her phone. If you wish, they can make private photos, but they will ask a lot of money for that. This information is 100% accurate. You deserve better than this woman. A full report will be ready by the end of the day."

A few hours later Vitaly added, "Please say nothing to her about the report. Keep everything confidential for one more day. It is very important. Oksana is now under investigation by the police."

Chapter Sixty

Vitlay's last message arrived a little too late. I had already confronted Oksana with the results of the report. I was overwhelmed by the information. I knew I had been ignoring her actions for too long, but this was much worse than I had ever imagined. There is no fool like an old fool.

I would have preferred to confront Oksana with the information face to face. Arguably, there should never have been a confrontation. Most people will say I should have simply blocked all communications with her and walked away. I will likely never understand why I didn't do that. Maybe by the time I am finished telling this story, I will have figured that out. I certainly hope so because it is incredible.

We were communicating primarily by email during this time. With the time difference and our schedules, it wasn't unusual for it to take twenty-four hours to receive a response from an email. This response took even longer. I could not imagine how Oksana would respond to the allegations. How could she address the issues? She had gotten good a lying, but this was cold hard evidence. It crossed my mind that I might never hear from her again. At the time, I thought that might be the best possible scenario.

But she did respond. She said, "I thought you cared about me! I knew someone was following me everywhere. But we are used to that in Ukraine. I am not living with anyone here. The man I was talking with is a policeman. He was asking me some questions and I was answering his questions. I am not a prostitute. I am a simple woman trying to survive in Ukraine. Now you have made me the object of an investigation by the Ukrainian police. Do you have any idea what can happen to people who are under investigation by the crooked police? No, you have no idea because you don't live in Ukraine; you live in America! How does it feel knowing you are responsible for this? Just leave me alone and tell the police to stop following me. I am not a criminal."

There was little doubt that Oksana was guilty as charged. There was little doubt that the pictures she had shown the investigators were photos I had taken of her at the Opera Hotel. It all came together. All of the pieces fit almost perfectly. And as badly as I felt about causing her all of these problems, I thought she deserved it.

And then, a few days later, I received an email from Oksana. I was so happy to hear that she wasn't in Siberia that I damn near forgot about the investigation. She apologized for the things she had said to me in her previous email. She told me I could never understand how the police work in Ukraine. They try to get something on the citizens so they can have absolute control of them. I had just made it easy for them.

Again, she told me she was not a prostitute. She said she was angry with me until she realized my investigation of her only proved how much I loved her. She didn't blame me for doing it. She forgave me!

Oksana was the best little liar I had ever seen. I had never even heard of anyone who could do it so well. Of course, the two reasons she was able to do such a great job were, she had a lot of practice and I loved her. I loved her and I felt so sorry for her. She was trying to survive virtually alone in a third-world country, and I had added to her woes. I wanted to go to Ukraine and hug the little whore.

If that sounds like I was conflicted, it's because I was. This is another one of those times when the reader will say this shit is too unbelievable. No relationship could survive this direct hit. I don't have the words to explain how we got through this period in the affair. There were times while this was going on I thought I could forgive her if I knew she had sold her body to survive. Then I would think I could never forgive her for lying to me for so long about so many things. But, in the end, we survived because I loved Oksana unconditionally and I thought there might be a way to make it to the finish line with her despite the incredible circumstances.

Slowly, day by day, we began to pick up the pieces. We were leaking oil, but surprisingly, we started talking about the future. We talked about how we must love each other because if we didn't, how could we have gotten through that terrible ordeal?

This was near the end of September 2016. On October 7, I boarded a plane for Kyiv. I didn't know if it was a case of love conquers all or just stupidity. I still don't know, but it's getting a little clearer with every word I write.

Chapter Sixty-One

This October trip was planned to last ten days. I couldn't get the Amsterdam connection, so I connected through Paris. The flight was pleasant and uneventful. Uneventful is a good thing when you are flying.

I have flown a lot and I have had some frightening experiences. Most of these bad experiences occurred when flying in relatively small planes. I think it's called General Aviation. On one occasion, the airport in Dothan, Alabama had to foam the runway because our nose gear failed to lower into position. The pilot did a masterful job of landing the King Air on its rear wheels. The aircraft came to rest at the end of the runway and gently tilted forward damaging the nose of the plane. But we were alive and that was the definition of a good landing.

There was a total of thirty individual flights in my five trips to Kyiv. There was not a single scary incident during those flights. There was some turbulence occasionally but that is to be expected. There was snow and ice in Ukraine, but the airport handled it well. Air travel is truly the safest way to travel in the twenty-first century. That's fortunate because I had no other choice.

All of these pleasant flying experiences made me much more comfortable. The results were that I was not as tired and jetlagged as on my first two trips. So, when I arrived, I didn't require as much rest before I was ready to resume normal activities. And "normal activities" with Oksana meant lots of sex.

Chapter Sixty-Two

The October trip was perfect. I arrived at the Opera Hotel a few hours before Oksana arrived by train from Kharkiv. That gave me a chance to get a shower and relax for a while in the hotel lobby with my favorite cocktail waitress in the world bringing Ukrainian chardonnay and chips.

When the bellman opened the two big front doors of the hotel and Oksana walked in, it was a wonderful sight. Of course, there was that toothpaste commercial smile, but there was also an excitement that I have seldom seen in my life. Everything bad that had happened recently suddenly vanished as if it had never happened. We never discussed any of it. It was simply gone with the wind.

Oksana never looked like she had just been on a Ukrainian passenger train for eight or nine hours. She looked great and she smelled edible. I honestly don't know how these Ukrainian women do it. It's their little magic act. I fall for it every time.

The bellman took her luggage to our room and Oksana joined me on one of the sofas in the lobby. She loved our daily wine and chips ritual in the hotel lobby as much as I did. After an hour in the lobby, we went directly to the room. It was obvious from our first kiss that food was not the primary issue on either of our minds.

When we got to our room the first thing, I did was remove my shoes as was expected. The second thing I did was remove everything Oksana was wearing. I don't recall ever being so hungry for a woman in my life. We tried to take our time, but it was hopeless. We consumed each other like we hadn't had sex for months. It was noisy and rough. It was loving and gentle. It was everything love-making is supposed to be and more. An hour or so later we ordered food from room service. It might be the best room service food in the world. Or maybe everything was so perfect that nothing could fuck it up.

After twenty minutes, a smiling lady brought our food and wine. We ate ravenously, just like we had made love. I hadn't realized I was so hungry. We shared our food and then I poured us a glass of good French wine and we sat down on the sofa and talked. When we had a language problem, we simply used the translator of the cellphone or the iPad. After a short while, this became second nature. It wasn't that inconvenient. Maybe it had to do with love.

About an hour later we were back in bed. The sex was slower this time but just as good as earlier. When we were done, we took a shower together and put on the bathrobes furnished by the hotel. Oksy insisted we take some pictures. Those pictures are no longer on my cellphone, but they are still on my computer. They are pictures of two of the happiest people in the world. It still tears my heart out every time I stumble onto one of them.

Chapter Sixty-Three

There were also pictures taken in the lobby of the hotel, the elevator, and the restaurant. Every spot was a perfect place for Oksana to make her usual "photo please," request.

The next day we went to one of our favorite restaurants. Piccolino was just as good as Northern Italian food got. Oksana wore her red dress, and she was stunning. I put on a sports coat so I wouldn't look so bad next to her. Of course, there were pictures of the event.

One of Oksana's favorite pictures was of our hands together in a taxi. We took dozens of these, and they were very romantic. We took a cab almost every day and there were plenty of photo opportunities. She had an eye for the perfect picture. It was her hidden talent. And, of course, she had lots of practice.

It is rather chilly in Kyiv in late October, and it was perfect weather for walking up and down the hilly terrain of the city. We took a long walk almost every day. There was a little juice bar up the hill about six blocks from the hotel and we walked there often. The juice was delicious.

While we were having our juice and coffee on our second day, we planned a day trip to the little town of Uman which was located about 210 kilometers south of Kyiv. Oksana wanted to show me a park there and I wanted to see what was outside the city of Kyiv. We contacted our guide Alex and told him we were going to rent a car and drive to Uman. He told us he was available, but we should hire a driver to take us there.

I immediately thought he was finding work for a friend. When I saw the condition of the "interstate" highway to Uman, I changed my mind.

There are a lot of expensive cars in Kyiv. You will see Mercedes, Porsche SUVs, Audis, and many other luxury cars. What you will not see are sports cars. A 911 Porsche wouldn't last a month. The roads are so bad the undercarriage would be destroyed.

The next day Alex and his driver picked us up at the hotel and we headed south. The highway to Uman was no better than the streets of Kyiv. There were potholes everywhere and dodging these made driving a very dangerous activity. Alex was right. A professional driver was a good decision. And I was shocked that the price was less than the cost of renting a car for the day.

On the way to Uman, we stopped by a little coffee shop and had some great Ukrainian coffee. These roadside shops weren't Starbucks. There were usually a couple of tables sitting in front of a small building. The lady took your order and brought you the coffee. It wasn't fancy, but the coffee was great.

It's only about 130 miles from Kyiv to Uman but it took us three hours to get there. There wasn't much traffic, but the road was terrible. I spent my entire career in highway construction, and I have never seen worse construction in my life than in Ukraine. I didn't think a paving machine could lay such a rough pavement. Oksana had a favorite saying, "Welcome to Ukraine." She used it several times on the way to Uman.

The park we were going to visit was Arboretum Sofiyivka, which was located on the northern side of the city. The park was huge, occupying about one square mile of real estate. It was truly a beautiful place to see. It was a gorgeous fall day, and a lot of people were taking advantage of the weather. We walked around for a couple of hours and ate lunch at a little café in the park. There were many opportunities for Oksana to say, "Photo please," and I almost always took her picture.

When we headed back to Kyiv, Alex stopped by a small convenience store and bought us all some beer. Fortunately, the driver declined. A beer in Ukraine isn't a 12-ounce bottle. I am certain it was in milliliters, but I would guess the bottle contained about a quart of beer. Ukrainian beer was good, and I was thirsty. About an hour out of Uman, I told Alex we would need to make a pit stop before too long. He told me we would stop at the next rest area. In about fifteen minutes the driver pulled over to some kind of shed beside the road. I told Alex it was fine with me if we waited until we reached the rest area. He said, "This is the rest area."

I was raised in the South and in the country, but I had never seen anything quite like this facility. I walked around a wall and saw a hole in the floor about six inches in diameter. Whatever you had to do was supposed to go into that hole. My first thought was that vomit was a likely candidate. The aim of the last few customers was not that good. It was on the floor and the walls. Fortunately, the beer made it possible to stand a few feet from the hole. I held my breath, did my business, and got out of there. I did take a picture of the facility. No one to whom I later showed the picture believed me when I told them this was a rest area. When we got back into the car, Oksana smiled and said, "Welcome to Ukraine."

Ukraine Interstate Rest Area

Chapter Sixty-Four

One would think that being confined to a single hotel room in a third-world country with anyone would get old. It did not. I have already said it was perfect, and perfect does not get old.

For ten glorious days, Oksana and I walked the streets of an Old Russian city and held hands. We made love at least once every day. We ate great food and drank good wine. I was never bored. Oksana often said it wasn't the real world. We were on a honeymoon. She was right, of course, but even a honeymoon would eventually grow old if there wasn't something special going on.

On the night of October 11, I asked Oksana if she would marry me. We had decided to apply for a K1-visa. This was commonly referred to as a fiancé visa. The term fiancé generally referred to a couple who was engaged to be married. So the logical question was, "Are we engaged to be married?" Oksana agreed that we were. I asked her if she wanted me to buy her an engagement ring and she said yes, so the next morning we went to Ocean Plaza and looked at rings.

Ukraine Brides and common sense told me to purchase a token engagement ring. That can be done for a hundred dollars. But since common sense didn't apply to love, we decided on the $1,200 model. I want to make it clear this was my decision. I firmly believe Oksana would have been perfectly happy with a much less expensive ring. And, as diamond rings go, this was not expensive.

After we shopped for the ring, we decided to celebrate at Vino e Cucina. We ordered a bottle of Veuve Clicquot and some good food. Of course, we took lots of pictures of Oksana's hands with her new ring. It was a night to remember. Unfortunately, later on, it would become a night that would be impossible to forget.

Chapter Sixty-Five

There is a television series on TLC about the K1-visa. The show is called *Ninety Day Fiancé*. I have watched almost every episode. Some of the content is just Hollywood, but most of it is accurate. The glaring issue I have with the show is they never explain how complicated the K1-visa process is. I understand it's more entertaining to talk about the emotional and sexual aspects of the process, but by dismissing the bureaucratic nightmare involved in the application, the show ignores a major part of the ordeal.

The petition for the fiancé visa is made through the United States Citizenship and Immigration Service (USCIS). USCIS is under the Department of Homeland Security. If approved, the alien applicant may travel to the U.S. and stay for ninety days. If the alien and her sponsor aren't married within those ninety days, the alien must leave the country.

It is possible to complete the K1-visa application without any assistance—I can't imagine how this could be done, but the government says it is possible. It reminds me of the old joke, "I'm with the IRS and I'm here to help you." When I called a friend in Washington, she recommended I contact an attorney in Birmingham to help with the process. She gave me the telephone number and I gave the attorney a call. She wasn't very friendly, and she wasn't encouraging. She told me she had plenty of work without messing with the fiancé visas and only helped people who were recommended by my friend in Washington. It made me feel so special.

The attorney asked me where I had met Oksana and I could imagine the smile on her face when I replied. She told me it would cost about $5,000 and there was no guarantee it would be approved. She asked me why I didn't just move to Ukraine. This was not going well. Then she told me, "You need to wrap your mind around a year to get all of this done." That was all I needed to hear. Do some people still think that everyone else is ignorant? Do they not know the internet has made formerly secret and valuable information readily available to everyone with a computer and an internet connection?

I had read a lot about the K1-visa, and I knew it was presently an approximate six-month process. I contacted an internet visa service called RapidVisa and determined the entire cost was about $1,200. RapidVisa was located in Las Vegas, Nevada. That made me nervous at first, but they did a great job guiding me through the complicated process and the K1-visa came in right on time.

It was an incredibly complicated process to get all of the documentation compiled in the proper form for submission to USCIS. If Oksana had not been located in Ukraine it would have been much easier. It takes a week or more to get a FedEx envelope from Ukraine to the U.S. All of the documents required an original signature and that took a lot of time.

Our application contained 52 pages of documents. This didn't include backup information that must be kept just in case the government wanted to see it. I am not going to list every document that is required—that information is available online—but I will mention just a few of the unusually detailed requirements of the application process.

All documents must be translated into English. The translator must sign an affidavit confirming the accuracy of the translation. All divorce decrees must be submitted. These must be translated into English. Each applicant must submit a letter of intent. I had to personally write Oksana's information "in her native language." We both had to submit proof of citizenship documentation.

RapidVisa worked with me for several weeks to make certain the application was completed accurately. The petition was received by USCIS on November 21, 2016. USCIS has a website where you can go to check on the progress of the application. You can even click on a link that gives you the current estimated processing time for various types of visa applications. I went there and saw it was five months. I received a notice of approval on March 31, 2017. That is four months and ten days from the date the application was received. I thought about sending a copy of the notice to the smart-ass lawyer in Birmingham, but it was just a passing thought.

The notice itself is a very official-looking green document that you would expect to come from the U.S. government. I was delighted that all of our hard work had paid off. There were women in Ukraine who would give everything they had for this free ticket to America. But this approved K1-visa would never be used by anyone.

Chapter Sixty-Six

The wonderful days and magical nights went on for ten days. On the night of October 13, Oksana told me she wanted us to go to an indoor skydiving center in town. This is a vertical wind tunnel where flying is simulated. I had done it many years ago and I agreed to let her try it. I never had any intention of doing it again myself.

Flying Oksana

It was cold as a son of a bitch when we got up on October 14. I thought this would save me, but Oksana was born and raised in the tundra, and she was hell-bent and determined to fly. So, with the wind blowing about 20 miles an hour and the temperature hovering around 40 degrees, we took a taxi to the wind tunnel. It took an hour for her to get suited up and trained. I have to admit she was cute in that flight suit. I took pictures of her training and her flight. She did the best of the half-dozen people in her group. She was so proud of herself. I was proud of her as well.

The next day, on October 15, we went shopping at Ocean Plaza. I had offered to buy Oksana some clothes. She rarely asked for anything, and I wanted to make her happy. We looked around the mall and she finally found something she liked at Tommy Hilfiger. She picked out a nice sweater and a pair of those blue jeans that are almost completed worn out. She also found a pair of black leather boots that looked great on her. After we returned to the hotel, she modeled everything for me. She wore her new clothes when we went to Café Room 88 for dinner. We stopped by Piccolino Restaurant on the way so I could take more pictures of her. I don't think she was ever happier than when she was in front of a camera.

The archived messages on Ukraine Brides ended on July 17. The days are fuzzy in my memory after then. There is little to jog my memory except for the many pictures on my computer. Fortunately, my iPhone put a date on those pictures. I was flying by the seat of my pants, but I had an electronic co-pilot.

Chapter Sixty-Seven

My flight home left early in the morning on October 17. As was her custom, Oksana took the taxi to the airport with me. She held my hand all the way. And, no matter what might happen to us later, we were in love during this period in our lives. There was no doubt then and there is little doubt now.

I now had all of Oksana's contact information, so beginning in July, we had begun to use Viber to communicate. Viber doesn't archive messages, so there is no way to determine how many messages we sent during the next nine months. The messaging is free. Some days we chatted for an hour or two. If I had to guess, I would estimate we sent at least 3,000 messages during that period. It sounds like a lot but it's only about 11 messages a day. Some days we sent a lot more than that.

Chatting with Oksana every day helped make our time apart a little less unbearable. She was busy and I took some trips to the coast to fish and relax. We immediately began planning our next meeting in Kyiv. We decided on the first three weeks of December. This was only six weeks away. Toward the end of the six weeks, we were missing each other badly and we decided we would never be apart for more than four weeks again.

Being engaged to be married made a lot of difference in our communications. We were almost always positive. We talked about making love and missing each other. And we talked about our future together. I was no longer the least bit interested in any other woman. Oksana was all I would need for the rest of my life. It was a huge burden off of our relationship. We were still 6,000 miles apart, but it was finally beginning to feel like something close to normal.

Chapter Sixty-Eight

Oksana often told me she loved me. When I mentioned our age difference, she would tell me her life expectancy was the same as mine because she didn't want to live without me. I thought this was a little beyond the pale. I certainly didn't want to even think of her dying with me. I wanted to imagine her having a happy life long after I was no longer around. But the thought sounded good to someone in love.

To even the casual observer, it would have been obvious we were in love. We were always holding hands and Oksana was not at all shy about public affection. But, considering all of the issues we had been through, there was always a scintilla of doubt in the back of my mind. On one occasion, she was telling me how much she loved me, and I told her I thought I might have fallen in love with her when we first met. She told me she didn't believe in love at first sight. Then I asked her on Viber how much she loved me.

She messaged me, "I am madly in love with you. I will always be with you."

I said to her, "If you will stay by my side, I can do anything. I have never had such a reason to live. Could you please tell me again how you finally fell in love with me?"

She replied, "I have told you that it was not love at first sight. I do not believe in this. It can only be a sexual attraction. First, I liked your appearance. Then, we chatted. When we met in a real meeting, it resolved all issues. It was your attitude toward me. It was the way you courted me and made me feel special. I felt your energy and your actions. I heard your words."

I told her, "I didn't think it was possible for us. It just seemed too crazy. But there was no doubt I fell in love with you when you jumped into my arms that first time at the Opera Hotel."

Oksana replied, "At that first meeting, you surprised me in bed. I was shocked by you. You know how important sex is for me. That was crucial for me. I decided then I wanted to pursue a relationship with you. The second meeting was even brighter. It was then that I decided I wanted to fly to you."

Oksana continued, "After you had me under surveillance, I understood you were madly in love with me, and I didn't care about the investigation. The third meeting was insane. I was more and more overwhelmed with emotion. Your love covered me from head to toe. I realized then I loved you madly. I knew I wanted to be with you forever. I was crying. Do you remember me crying? I knew you would be a good husband, a friend, protector, and lover. With you, I feel like a real, satisfied, and happy woman. For you, I am ready to go to the end of the world! I still can't believe all of these important qualities could be found in one man."

I was overcome with emotion when I heard this. I told her my family and friends were looking forward to the wedding. We had discussed a small wedding, but I told her it might be getting out of hand. She said, "Are people getting in line for our wedding? That is good! We will surprise everyone with our great love. We will discuss everything but the final decision about the size of the wedding will be yours."

It was late in Ukraine, and we said goodnight. The following morning Oksana sent me another message. She wrote, "Yesterday I did not finish my story about our love. At every meeting with you, I began to admire and understand you more and more. Every day I was more and more in love with you. Being apart from you only intensifies my feelings. I am so proud of you. You are my universe. I thank God that he gave me you. I am madly in love with you and I want to be near you always!"

I couldn't remember hearing anything so beautiful in my life. All of my doubts disappeared in her cloud of words.

Chapter Sixty-Nine

The flight to Kyiv was a twenty-hour ordeal but it was becoming easier every time. I was reading some good books during this period and that helped. I was also able to sleep on the night flights and that significantly shortened the trip.

When I left Amsterdam, I took some pictures out the window of the plane. The huge green fields were beautiful. When the plane landed three hours later in Kyiv, everything was solid white.

I was born and raised in Florida, but I have been to cold places. I was in New York City attending a business seminar early in my career and I damn near froze to death in the worst blizzard there in ten years.

I don't know what I was doing out there on the street under those conditions, but I soon noticed almost no one else was that crazy. I wasn't dressed for the wind and temperature, and I was quickly in trouble. I rounded a corner and visibility was near zero.

The wind was gusting to around 40 miles an hour. I have no idea how I stumbled into that bar, but some would call it a miracle. I ordered an Irish coffee and asked the bartender to call me a taxi. It took the Yellow Cab an hour to get through the storm to the bar. That's a lot of Irish coffee. I made it back to the New York Hilton. I had learned a valuable lesson about the weather that I would never forget.

Winter in central Ukraine was not about strolling down the sidewalk hand in hand. It was about staying inside until you have to go out for wine or to treat cabin fever. I have no idea why people submit themselves to this torture. Do they not understand there are other places on the planet where survival isn't a constant issue?

I must admit Kyiv is a beautiful city after a fresh snowfall. The snow covers the ugly and it truly is lovely. Then the cars turn the beautiful white stuff into slush. The white becomes a shade of gray that almost perfectly matches the buildings. I know most people have experienced all of this, but I live in the south of the U.S., and I had almost forgotten just how hostile weather can be.

The locals were talking about how mild the winter was. The temperature never rose above freezing and the wind was almost always blowing in your face. How could it get much worse? Yes, I know that this sounds like a walk that is uphill both ways, but I am just reporting my perception here.

Chapter Seventy

Oksana arrived at the Opera Hotel a couple of hours before me. The hotel had arranged for my usual airport pickup and the driver had no problem with the weather conditions. That amount of snow and ice would have shut down the city of Birmingham, Alabama. The stores would have run out of bread and milk, and the kids would not be going to school. International travel is good for many reasons. It broadens you intellectually. It also reduces your natural urge to panic when the weather changes.

When I arrived at the Opera, I was greeted warmly by the staff. The prodigal son had returned. That might be a little hyperbolic, but I was a good tipper and I think that might be unusual in Ukraine. Oksana was always shocked when I left a twenty percent tip for excellent service. I think it's the right thing to do and it pays dividends.

I couldn't wait to get in the elevator and go to the room. I told the front desk clerk I would check in later. She understood. See what I mean about tipping?

When Oksana opened the door to our room, she jumped into my arms. This little woman was unaware of her own strength. She was hugging and kissing me like a wild woman. She was biting me again. She had perfect teeth and she was using them. Her biting sometimes drew blood. And it hurt like hell. Oksana was borderline sadomasochistic. I don't understand this but I got used to slapping her on her butt, hitting her softly with my belt, and acting a little rough. I could never bring myself to do much else. I could never physically hurt a woman no matter what turned her on. I just couldn't do it.

After our painful introduction, I walked into the room, and I immediately noticed the bed. Oksana had used rose petals to form the shape of a large pink heart in the middle of the bed. It was one of the most romantic things I had ever seen. When she saw the expression on my face, I could tell she was pleased. Gifts when people meet are critical in Ukraine. This was her gift to me. She was delighted with my reaction.

To complete the gift, Oksana took off all of her clothes and positioned herself in the middle of the rose petals. Naturally, her first words were, "Photo please." I gladly complied. Those pictures will eventually be deleted from my laptop, but I'm not ready for that just yet.

What followed was just too personal and intimate to share. We had been apart for six weeks and it was apparent neither of us had had sex during that time. We did everything we could think of for each other. When we were done an hour and a half later, the room smelled of sex and roses. It was as close to Heaven as I would ever get.

We ordered some food and wine from room service. When the young lady came to make the delivery, she had a shy smile on her face. I knew the hotel staff was having a field day with our story. An older man and a beautiful young woman; what could be more interesting?

The very next night, Oksana and I had begun making out on the sofa in the room. Then she had purposefully thrown us on the floor for sex. We were between the sofa and the coffee table when the young woman who serviced the mini bars came in the door.

She may have rung the bell. My hearing isn't great, and Oksana was in the middle of an orgasm and didn't give a damn. The young woman smiled, quietly said, "excuse me," and slowly left the room. Oksana never acknowledged anything had happened.

I can remember when a couple caught in the act would have been very embarrassed as they jumped up off the floor and looked for their clothes immediately. That was not even a consideration here. I was a little shocked, but it was an event we relished and often talked about.

The sofa from which Oksana threw us to the floor

It was also an event the hotel staff often talked about. Wherever we went in the hotel after that night, virtually every employee of the hotel looked at us differently. There was the knowing smile and the extra special attention they paid us.

I am beginning to think writing a book isn't as cathartic as I had hoped it would be. Fuck this.

Chapter Seventy-One

Three weeks is a long time to be in a single room with one person. After a while, you tend to become cellmates. The winter conditions had the potential of making things much worse. But this simply did not happen.

We often walked to the grocery store a few blocks from the hotel to purchase wine and special food that we both liked. We also walked to our favorite restaurants in the area. Café Room 88 was our everyday choice because Oksana was concerned about spending so much on food. But I insisted we eat at Piccolino occasionally because the food was world-class, and the tab was about half what I was used to paying in the States.

On the evening of December 5, we decided to walk down the hill to Piccolino for dinner. I had grown accustomed to the great food there, but I wasn't expecting anything extraordinary. I was in for a surprise.

The enjoyment of wine is a function of several factors. The wine must be good, of course. But just as important is the atmosphere. I am not a big fan of Bordeaux wine, but when I was visiting a winery there several years ago, I had lunch on the property. The food was delicious, and you could see the vineyards through the windows in the little winery café. It was a special meal, and the atmosphere was incredible. When I returned home, I purchased a case of the same wine and it was good, but it was never as good as it was with that meal in Bordeaux.

After we ordered our meal, the Piccolino sommelier came to our table to recommend a wine to complement our choices. He picked a Pinot Grigio. I like the wine, but it would not have been my first choice. I told him this, but he persisted. I agreed to taste the wine. He brought a small sample of the wine in a large glass. This guy knew what he was doing. The way to turn a $20 bottle of wine into a $40 bottle of wine is to double the size of the glass. The change in taste is shocking.

When I tasted the wine, I was blown away. I asked to see the bottle. I took a picture and ordered the wine. It was a 2012 Fantinel Pinot Grigio. I had never heard of it. I have tried repeatedly to purchase the wine in the U.S., but I can't find it here. It likely doesn't matter. It wasn't just the wine. It was the moment. It was the atmosphere. It was Oksana.

Chapter Seventy-Two

The following day, Oksana and I were in the hotel room when we got into a little shoving match. I don't remember what started it, but it did happen occasionally. I do recall that I had gone into the bathroom to brush my teeth and Oksana had decided to lock me in there. The actual lock on the door is operated from the inside so she had to improvise. She wedged something under the door and put her full weight and considerable strength against the door.

I am slightly claustrophobic, so I didn't handle this well. I pushed with all of my strength but couldn't budge the door. I assumed she had somehow moved the heavy chest in front of the door. In desperation, I ran against the door, shoulder first. She timed it perfectly. She opened the door just as I made contact. The result was I was sprawled out on the floor of the foyer, feeling and looking like a fool. Oksana could not stop laughing. I was a little pissed off but I couldn't help but laugh with her.

She was so proud of herself for outsmarting me that she kept re-enacting the scene over and over. She was down on the floor trying to look like me in my most embarrassing moment. Tears were streaming down her cheeks. She could hardly catch her breath. We were both laughing. I took a couple of pictures of her on the floor. It was a Kodak moment.

Kodak moments were Oksana moments. I never understood her obsession with photos of herself. Maybe it was because she was so damned photogenic.

That smile was captivating. Ukraine Brides had seen her potential and they were right.

But it wasn't just photography that interested Oksana. Her interests ran the gamut. She had an insatiable desire to experience everything. She had been limited in her ability to explore the world and I think she saw that was possible with me. I was still surprised when she told me she wanted to go to a firing range and shoot some guns. I asked her what kind of guns she wanted to shoot, and she said, "I want to shoot them all."

So, we took a taxi through the snow to a public firing range in the center of the city. It was located in a surprisingly modern high-rise building with ultra-modern décor. We had called ahead, and they were expecting us.

I am nervous when I am in a foreign country and other people have guns and I don't. When I visited Cuba several years ago, I never got used to what looked to me like kids walking the streets with AK-47s. If someone had said, 'boo," I felt they could easily reel off a few rounds and then say, "Hey, I'm sorry."

The young man who was our instructor and guide was very nice and knowledgeable. He spoke Russian and a little English. He showed us the available firearms and the ammunition for each gun. He told us how much each round would cost and talked a lot about safety. I began to relax a bit. Americans tend to think people from other countries aren't so smart. I might have fallen into that trap.

I recommended to Oksana that she stay with the handguns for her first shooting session. She agreed. She was shown some Russian and Ukrainian semiautomatic pistols. I was still a little nervous, but this guy knew his shit. Oksana picked out a couple of handguns and he went over the procedure for loading and firing the guns.

Oksana at the firing range in Kyiv

Oksana was not at all intimidated by the weapons. I guess when you are raised with the sound of gunfire in the distance you get used to the concept. She pointed the automatic weapon down range and pulled the trigger. The recoil was apparent. She looked at me and smiled. For some reason, it occurred to me how fragile life could be. She returned her attention to the target and emptied the clip directly into the silhouette. Shit.

I have owned guns my entire life. I like revolvers because they are more predictable than automatics. But I liked the looks of the Ukrainian automatic and decided to fire a couple of clips through it. I had no problem putting every round in the target. Oksana was impressed, but she wasn't as impressed as I was. I had never seen a woman less intimidated by a gun.

Chapter Seventy-Three

Our December meeting was looking like a repeat performance of our October meeting. We were making love regularly and we managed to get out of the hotel every day for some reason. We had some minor disagreements, but we were happy together and life was good.

On December 11, we went back to Piccolino for dinner. Oksana preferred Café Room 88 but I couldn't wait to see if the Fantinel Pinot Grigio was as good as I thought it was or if our previous experience had been an anomaly. Again, the wine was outstanding.

Piccolino had begun to give Oksana and me a little gift each time we left the restaurant. This was a part of the Ukrainian tradition of giving gifts. It was everywhere. But tonight, the sommelier brought us a bottle of Limoncello they make at the restaurant. This drink is a combination of lemons, vodka, water and sugar.

There may be some secret stuff, but these are the essential ingredients. This version was delicious. We drank the entire bottle of Limoncello and returned to the hotel.

Chapter Seventy-Four

The Opera Hotel was our home. Whatever Oksana and I did during the day, when we returned to the Opera, we were home. It was warm and inviting. The people there liked us and we liked them. Everything anyone needed was there under one roof. I have often wondered if I could live in an environment like that. I think I could.

The hotel was decorated for Christmas. There was a huge Christmas tree in the lobby and the outside was beautiful in the winter snow. I took pictures of our early evenings in the lobby with our glasses of chardonnay and chips. It was unforgettable.

The spa at the Opera was very nice. You could get all of the usual services there. There was a good workout room, and the Jacuzzi and sauna were never crowded.

When Oksana and I were in the Jacuzzi on the evening of December 16, there was no one else in the area but for us. She wanted me to take some sexy pictures of her in every conceivable pose. We had brought a bottle of red wine from the mini bar in the room, but that was not the reason she was so sensual. She was always sensual.

After a dozen pictures, Oksana wanted me to take some more pictures of her giving me a blowjob. It was difficult to concentrate on photography when a lovely woman had your penis in her mouth, but I was willing to give it a try. The things you do for love. I took several photos of her, but she wasn't satisfied. Okay, I can finally come clean. I wasn't giving it my best effort.

Chapter Seventy-Five

I don't know how many Americans go to the theater, but I would guess there are more people who handle snakes than have ever been to see a Puccini opera. We just don't give a damn about the arts. Hell, we don't even know what "the arts" means. We tend to think a hamburger and French fries are the finer things of life. The result is obvious.

In Europe, people from every walk of life put a lot of emphasis on the arts. When there is a famous opera singer in town the place is packed, and the people leave with tears in their eyes. They might not understand a word of the Italian language, but they understand they have witnessed something special.

The Kyiv Opera group was established in 1867. The National Opera House of Ukraine is located in the city of about five blocks from the Opera Hotel. There are opera groups in all major Ukrainian cities.

On December 18, the Spanish tenor Jose Carreras was in town for a performance. It wasn't an opera performance, but he was singing some opera songs along with some Christmas carols. Carreras is particularly known for his performances in the operas of Puccini and Verdi. He became an opera superstar as one of the Three Tenors along with Placido Domingo and Luciano Pavarotti. People who had never heard opera became interested because of the beauty of the music of the trio.

I asked the concierge to see if he could get us last-minute tickets to the Carreras event. He worked his usual magic and we soon had great tickets to the show. Oksana was as excited as a little girl at Christmas. Come to think of it, that's exactly what she was.

The night of December 18, was one of the coldest of the year. Fortunately, there was little wind, and it didn't feel as cold as it had been since the beginning of the month. Oksana was stunning in her red dress and fur coat. I must have taken two dozen pictures of her excluding ones of us together at the hotel and the show. We arrived early so we could watch the people come in dressed to the nines. We weren't disappointed. Of course, some people go to the opera in jeans now, but most wear their very best clothes. We had a glass of wine at the theater, bought a program, and waited for the show to begin.

I am not a big fan of Christmas carols, likely because we begin playing them in the U.S. every year in October, but the stage was beautifully decorated for the season and these people could sing. I don't recall the name of the soprano who performed but she kicked Jose's butt. She was one of the best I had ever heard. When she sang the Puccini aria "O Mio Babbino Caro," she brought the house down. As I am writing this, I can hear Maria Callas singing this aria and it affects me greatly. I have heard it a hundred times and the emotional effect is almost always the same.

For many reasons, this had been a day to remember. Oksana and I had eaten lunch at Café Room 88, attended a great show, and stopped by the grocery store to pick up some mozzarella tomato salad ingredients. This is one of Oksana's favorite meals and the ingredients were amazingly fresh considering the time of the year. We ate the salad and drank a bottle of good

French white wine we had picked up at the grocery store.

When we were finished with dinner, Oksana mentioned we had skipped a day making love. She told me a day without sex made her frustrated and on edge. When she asked if we were going to have sex, I said yes, of course. When she looked at the time on her cellphone, she saw that it was just past midnight. She said, "Look, we have now gone two days without sex!" I thought she was kidding.

I told Oksana I would clean up the dinner mess while she got ready to go to bed. We almost always ate out, but in the room, I usually prepared the meal, and we shared the cleanup chore. She seemed a little stressed and I thought the bathroom time might settle her down.

We got in bed around 12:30. I was soon doing one of my favorite things—giving Oksana oral sex. Surprisingly, after about forty minutes she had not had a single noticeable orgasm. And her orgasms are very noticeable. I asked if she wanted me to get the vibrator. She shrugged. Something was on her mind. I got up and got the vibrator from the bathroom. At about 1:40 she still had not climaxed. It had been a long day. I was exhausted. When I paused for a five-minute break, Oksana grabbed the cover, jerked it over her head, and went fast asleep. There would be no more sex tonight. I had absolutely no idea what had happened.

Oksana possesses those great Ukrainian traits of stoicism and the ability to compartmentalize. I am not so blessed. I went into the bathroom and thought about what had happened. I even wrote some notes on my cellphone so I wouldn't forget the details. Memories will play tricks on your mind. I never understood what happened. It was likely some emotional issues with which she was dealing. It could be that women are from Venus. Whatever the cause, I thought what she did was very childish and immature. It would not be the last time I observed this type of behavior.

The next morning, we discussed what had happened. Oksana told me I should have held her, and everything would have been fine. She may very well have been right. But something told me she was just trying to blame everything that had happened on me. I began to wonder if there were issues, she wasn't sharing with me. I might have been slightly paranoid at the time but there was soon further evidence of potential problems in our relationship.

I have mentioned that one purpose of all this storytelling is to help me sort out the various issues. This event was one such issue. In retrospect, I can see I was overanalyzing everything. All of us have several thoughts going on at once, but that is no excuse. Oksana was correct. I should have been more understanding and supportive during her period of homesickness. I just couldn't see this at the time. And it was a time-turning point in our relationship.

Chapter Seventy-Six

There are no perfect relationships. There will always be issues that arise and will have to be resolved. The success of any emotional partnership depends on the willingness and the ability of the couple to work through the issues effectively. Oksana and I had cleared some rather high hurdles, but just because we had been effective in handling the huge issues didn't mean we were home free with the day-to-day problems.

One other matter that we were beginning to deal with from time to time was Oksana's temper. She was a sweet little Ukrainian lady, but she had a short fuse. There were times when she simply could not control it.

Oksana had found this store near the hotel that carried her brand of makeup. I thought it was all about the same. I was wrong. We got in a taxi and headed out to the store, but Oksana couldn't seem to find the place.

We rode up and down the same streets for twenty minutes. She was carrying on a very friendly conversation with the cab driver. They were having a wonderful time looking for this store and I was paying the fare for riding in circles. I didn't understand much of what they were saying but I did understand I wasn't going to do this for long. I finally said, "Oksana, why don't we find out where this place is located and come back tomorrow?"

She looked at me and shouted, "NO! We are going to find the store today!"

I don't react well to people who shout at me. I am particularly sensitive when I am yelled at in public. But I said nothing. We found the store. I waited in the taxi and Oksana went in alone. In fifteen minutes, she returned to the cab with her purchase. She was smiling. When we returned to the hotel, I sat down on the sofa in the room and asked her to sit down with me. I told her how I felt about her screaming at me in front of others. She apologized, said she understood, and that it wouldn't happen again. That was easy.

Two days later, she did almost the same thing in another cab. Immediately, she turned and smiled at me. I knew she remembered our conversation on the sofa in the hotel room. She also recalled her promise to control her temper in public, but she just couldn't do it. It had happened before she could think. It is a part of the Ukrainian culture, but it was also a part of Oksana's personality.

Chapter Seventy-Seven

We had applied for a K1-visa for Oksana to come to the U.S. for ninety days. Ukrainian citizens can also apply for a tourist visa. That visa can be processed in just a few days. Earlier on in this December trip, we had decided to apply for the tourist visa. What could it hurt? Even if we were denied we still had the K1 in process.

It is difficult to communicate with the U.S. Embassy in Kyiv. You can call and you might get connected to a human being or you might not. Even when you get connected you are told to go to the internet and follow the instructions. It looked complicated and it was expensive, but we decide to go for it.

The application was simple compared to the K1 petition. There was a passport picture required but I was able to cut and paste one of the pictures I had on my iPad onto the application. When we had finished, I thought it looked good. When we submitted the application online, we received an acknowledgement that it had been received and everything look fine. We celebrated our ingenuity.

A couple of days later, I received an email notifying us of the appointment the following day at the U.S. Embassy. Oksana was nervous but excited. We went over the questions the embassy would likely ask her and she did a good job of answering them. Ukrainian people don't seem to get too uptight about things and Oksana thought she could convince anyone of anything. I was certainly in no position to argue with her. I was a perfect example.

It was a ten-minute cab ride from the hotel to the U.S. Embassy. The building was indistinguishable from a prison. I took some pictures of the building just to show my friends back home how brave I was. There is a word that fits better, but I think brave is the word I used. It was snowing a little, the temperature was well below freezing, and the wind was blowing about fifteen miles an hour. Even the locals looked cold.

The line formed outside. It was like the U.S. was telling these aliens that if you want to come to America, you have to pay the price. If you don't like standing outside in the cold, you can just go back home. But they weren't going back home. There was a long line and Oksana smiled and got in it. She wanted me to take her picture. She was wearing a light grey fur coat with a hood. She was lovely standing there. I was freezing. I could not go in with her, so after she was inside the prison, I walked down the street looking for a coffee shop.

Freezing wind will find the path of least resistance. I can't remember ever being so cold. I walked into the wind because the prospects for coffee were better in that direction. I walked four or five blocks but there was nothing. I turned back toward the embassy and spotted a little butcher shop that was open. I stepped inside. It was warm and the lady behind the counter smiled at me. I was in Heaven. I asked, in my broken Russian, if she had any coffee. She poured me a cup of that wonderful Ukrainian coffee. She charged me about fifty cents. I drank it slowly and ordered another cup. I hung out in the butcher shop for about forty-five minutes. Then I went back to the embassy because I wanted to be there when Oksana came out. They wouldn't let her have her cellphone in the building and we had no way of communicating. I shouldn't have worried because I had to wait for her another thirty minutes outside the embassy. I walked up and down the sidewalk to keep from freezing.

When Oksana walked out into the cold, I knew instantly her application had been turned down. She showed me the rejection letter. The embassy made it very clear they rejected her application because they felt there was no compelling reason for her to return to Ukraine. Forget about family. Forget about the love of country. She was unemployed and that was all they needed. It had been a waste of time and money.

Ukrainian people are stoic. They have a saying that goes something like, "Life is a lesson; we will have learned it when it's over."

As I am writing this, a terrorist has thrown a bomb over the fence into the U.S. Embassy in Kyiv. He must have been standing on the very sidewalk where I was pacing up and down. It's early June. The rotten bastard should have tried it in the middle of winter. Terrorists are such chicken shit cowards.

Chapter Seventy-Eight

The day before I left, I received an email alert from the U.S. Embassy. I don't like receiving alerts from my government. It makes me as nervous as a whore in church. I have never received a good alert from Uncle Sam. Well, I did once receive a notice that I was due a tax refund, but that only meant I had overpaid my taxes in the first place.

The message said there was a demonstration planned for the next day in Kyiv. Some 30,000 demonstrators were expected to assemble in a park near our hotel. It further warned some violence was anticipated and one group had threatened to place bombs along the parade route. This was just fucking perfect.

I am not going to explain the purpose of the planned demonstration for two reasons. I didn't know and I didn't give a damn. I only cared about getting to the airport without getting killed or wounded. I know this sounds a bit dramatic, but I guess it depends on your perspective. I was in Ukraine. Where are you?

Oksana told me this kind of thing goes on all the time in Ukraine and there was nothing to worry about. This was coming from a woman who sometimes hears gunfire and the sound of bombs exploding in the distance. Please forgive me if I don't respect her judgment. She is thinking I'm a pussy again and I am beginning to feel a little feminine.

I had a conversation with the concierge about the taxi ride to the airport and he advised me to allow some extra time for the trip. What I wanted to hear him say was, "You don't have to worry about a thing. These demonstrations are never as serious as they sound." But he didn't say that. One factor I had in my favor was the time of my flight. I had to leave the hotel around 7:00 a.m. and no one thought the demonstrators would be up that early. Demonstrators are generally rather lazy about things other than demonstrating, so they aren't accustomed to getting out of bed early.

Oksana and I were up late, as we usually were on the night before my departure. We ordered a great bottle of Chablis and some good food from room service. We made love for a long time, and we took some erotic pictures that were rather nice. The best ones were a picture of my hand on various parts of Oksana's body. She has some lovely body parts and the pictures showed them perfectly. I still have these on my laptop, but I will soon delete them. At least, that is my plan.

I was exhausted, but I didn't sleep very well that night. We got up early and I called for a bellman. We were in the cab on the way to the airport by 6:45 a.m. Three blocks from the hotel there was cab driver standing in the middle of the street holding up his hand and motioning for our driver to stop. They were shouting to each other in Russian. I couldn't understand a word they were saying, and Oksana looked nervous. Our cab driver backed up half a block and made a right turn down an alley. Halfway down the alley, the traffic was backed up for several blocks. Our driver did a U-turn and headed in the opposite direction. That way was clear, and we were able to detour around whatever was blocking our departure. Soon we were on the main road that led to the airport.

It looked to me like it had rained during the night, but Oksana explained that the temperature had risen above freezing and the snow was melting. The windshield wipers were moving back and forth across the windshield of the cab and my heart rate was beginning to slow down to something approaching a normal rate. Welcome to Ukraine.

Chapter Seventy-Nine

When I returned to Birmingham, Oksana and I had already begun planning our next meeting. I was a little surprised when she told me she wanted me to meet her parents. She had talked with them, and they agreed to go to Kyiv for the meeting. It wasn't an easy trip from the east side of Ukraine to Kyiv. It was a five-hour drive and an eight-hour train ride. And there was no doubt that Russian military activity in the area was adding stress to the journey.

Within three weeks of my return home, I was back in an airplane and on my way to Ukraine. I arrived on January 14, 2017, and everything was white. The weather in Kyiv is brutal in January, but I had somewhat gotten used to the conditions.

Oksana had arrived at the Opera Hotel just before I got there. I had asked the hotel concierge to purchase a big bouquet of roses for her and have them available when I arrived at the hotel. The florist had done an outstanding job on the roses, and they looked perfect. When Oksana opened the door to the room I gave her the flowers, and she was overcome with joy. A gift is a magic trick in Ukraine.

For some reason, I was unusually exhausted from the trip, but I wasn't too tired to make passionate love to my fiancé and take her picture holding her roses in almost every conceivable pose. We ordered some room service food and a bottle of the Ukrainian chardonnay I had been missing for three weeks. After dinner, we drank our wine and discussed the upcoming meeting with her parents.

It quickly became obvious the meeting with her parents was more than I had envisioned. I was thinking we would meet and have dinner and that would be about it. But that isn't the way it's done in Ukraine. She wanted us to meet her parents at the train station and take a taxi back to the hotel together. After her parents rested, Oksana had planned a dinner for all of us in the early evening of their arrival. The next day she wanted me to get a private room for a mid-afternoon meal where we would reenact our engagement ceremony. When I say ceremony, I mean down on one knee in front of her parents and the world. I know this is considered traditional throughout the world, but it is essential in Ukraine. I had no problem with this request. I loved Oksana and I wanted everyone to know it.

When I learned of Oksana's elaborate plans, I immediately thought of the small engagement ring I had bought her. The ring was fine for our private purposes, but I would have been embarrassed to present it to her in a more formal ceremony. I thought her parents might think I wasn't very serious about their daughter. I thought it might send the wrong message.

Oksana told me the small ring would be just fine, but I insisted that we try to trade it in for a larger model. She finally agreed and we returned to the Ocean Plaza jewelry store where we had bought the small ring. The store clerk told us the ring could not be traded in but she could weigh it and give us the value of the gold off the purchase of another ring. That would have been about $75. I didn't say a word.

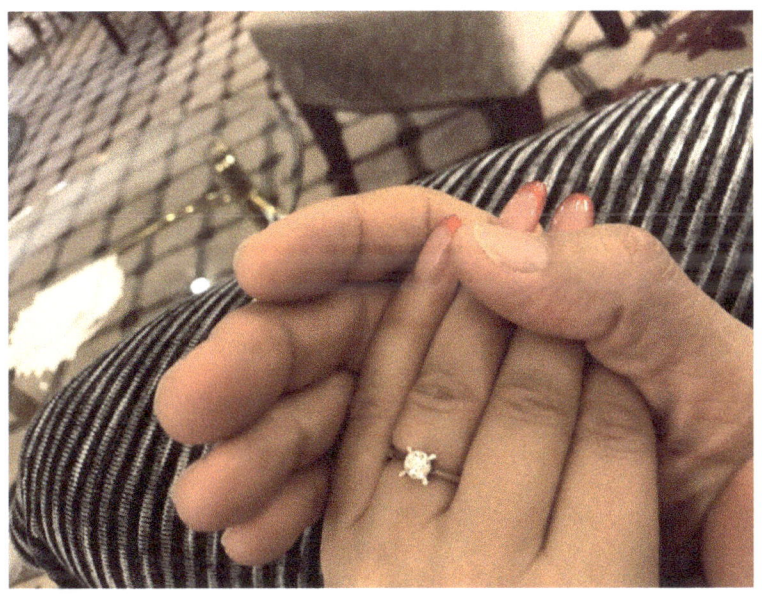
Oksana's replacement engagement ring

I picked up the ring and walked out of the store. We went to another store in the mall, and they told us the same thing. Welcome to Ukraine.

At the third store, we found a ring with a half-carat diamond that was beautiful on Oksana's little hand. The price was $6,000. We didn't even mention trading in the small ring.

Chapter Eighty

On the evening of January 16, Oksana and I met her parents at the train station. I should have been more observant about the custom of meeting people and seeing them off. It would be a mistake I would live to regret.

Her parents were both smiling when they saw us. Her father was carrying a package. He gave it to me. It was a present from Oksana to me. I was surprised.

Oksana's parents were very pleasant people, and it was obvious this was not going to be difficult at all. Of course, they spoke only Russian, but I had gotten used to being patient with communications and this was never a big problem for me. We took a taxi back to the hotel and I gave Oksana's mother a bouquet the concierge had purchased for me. I was learning.

I had already checked her parents into the hotel. Her mother was tired so they went to their room immediately. We agreed to meet in the lobby in two hours and go to dinner. Oksana wanted to take her parents to Café Room 88, and I readily agreed.

When Oksana and I got to our room I opened my gift from her. She had hired an artist to paint my portrait from a photograph of me standing next to my Harley Davidson motorcycle somewhere in Canada. I had no idea where I would hang it, but that wasn't the point. No one had ever given me a more intimate and personal gift in my life. I was overcome with emotion. We sat together on the floor looking at the picture for a long time. It led to some very special, unforgettable lovemaking. I will leave the details to your imagination.

A little later, we ate the usual good food at Oksana's favorite café and had a great conversation with her mom and dad. We used the Google Translator application on our cellphones. Her parents were very impressed. They had been worried we wouldn't be able to communicate at all, but they were now pleased and much more relaxed.

When we finished dinner, we took the ten-minute walk back to the Opera Hotel. We sat on the sofas in the lobby and had a glass of wine. It was obvious her parents were tired from their long day. We said goodnight and went up to our rooms.

Chapter Eighty-One

We didn't see Oksana's parents again the following morning. They had gone to the spa, and we had gone to the gym to work out. The gym was near the spa, but we had somehow missed them.

Earlier we contacted the hotel events manager, and she showed us a couple of rooms that were available for our engagement lunch. Both of us thought the rooms were too cold for the ceremony and we decided to use the main restaurant. At 3:00 p.m., there would not be many people in the restaurant and there was a corner that was somewhat private.

It turned out to be a great choice. There were only two couples in the restaurant when we arrived. The staff had arranged a large table in the corner of the beautiful restaurant, and they had placed some flowers on our table. There must have been a half dozen staff members waiting on us and they were all smiling. Everyone knew what was about to happen.

I had brought more flowers for Oksana's mother, and I had arranged for Vlada to be there to help us communicate. I ordered champagne and the ceremony officially began.

There were toasts and more champagne. We ate lunch and talked. One thing Oksana's mother said that I will never forget was, "When I came here I had a hundred questions for you. After I met you, I have no questions." It was one of the nicest things anyone ever said about me.

When it came time for me to give Oksana the ring, I turned to her father and told him I first wanted to make some promises to him regarding his daughter. I told him I would take care of her in every way. I told him I would honor and respect her for the rest of my life. I promised I would never hurt her in any way and that she could come to Ukraine regularly to visit her family. Maybe it was the champagne, but there were tears in his eyes. It was a very touching scene.

When I got down on one knee and faced Oksana, I saw her smile and the rest was easy. I told her everything I had told her father. I paused for Vlada to repeat every sentence. When I placed the ring on Oksana's finger there wasn't a dry eye in the room with one exception. Oksana just smiled—she didn't shed a tear.

Vlada took a lot of pictures of us. The restaurant was beautiful, there were a lot of flowers, and the pictures were beautiful. Things could not have gone more perfectly.

That evening the manager of the Opera Hotel sent a personal letter to our room. The letter congratulated Oksana and me on our engagement and wished us every success in our upcoming marriage. This was a classy hotel.

The next morning Oksana's parents were leaving, and we met in the lobby for coffee and to see them off. Ukrainian people are very affectionate when you get to know them. I had gotten to know her mom and dad during the past two days, and I was beginning to feel they had accepted me into the family.

Oksana and I spent the next few days basking in the bliss of our official engagement. I was so pleased that I had bought her the larger ring. We must have taken a hundred pictures of her hand with that ring on her finger.

Of course, there were many other pictures taken throughout the hotel too. She was very happy. We were both happy. But soon it was time to leave again, and this event was getting more difficult every time we did it. We knew we were several months away from getting the visa approved, and the time apart was beginning to become cruel and unusual punishment.

Chapter Eighty-Two

The taxi ride to the airport was somber. It was cold and there was a little snow coming down. As usual, Oksana rode with me to the airport and we had breakfast at the café there. We stayed together until the last minute for me to get to my gate. The line at customs was short, but you never know how long the process might take. What happened next was the nightmare that had been in the back of my mind since my first trip to Ukraine many months ago but had never happened. I had forgotten that anything bad could happen. I was immune. That was about to change.

When I placed my passport on the counter, the border officer asked, "Are you a Ukrainian citizen?" His English was not good, but I understood the question clearly.

I replied, "No, I am a U.S. citizen."
He then said the last words I wanted to hear from a Ukrainian official. "Please follow me."

I followed him to a small room just down the hallway from the border checkpoint. He closed the door. There was a woman in the room working on a computer. He told me to sit down. My heart was beating fast.

My plane was leaving in twenty minutes. I knew I had done nothing wrong, but I didn't think that mattered much at this point. The border officer was young, and he had a gun. I was clearly at his mercy.

He said to me in broken English, "You have been in Ukraine for more than nineteen days." I told him I had been in Ukraine for only seven days. He said, "You have been in Ukraine for more than nineteen days in the last 180 days."

I replied, "Yes, I have been in Ukraine for about 60 days during the past 180 days. Is that a problem?"
He said, "It is a big problem when you have been in Ukraine for more than nineteen days."

I was confused. I was sweating. I told him my plane was leaving in five minutes. He replied, "Your plane is not my problem or your problem at this moment." I thought about all of the money I had spent in his country during the past few months, but I didn't say a word about that. I just wanted to get out of that room, get on my flight, and get the hell out of Ukraine. I told him, "Please tell me what I need to do to correct my mistake."

He said, "You must pay a fine." Now I understood. This was a simple shakedown. I asked the amount of the fine. He told me in Ukrainian currency, but I quickly converted that to U.S. dollars. The fine was about $80, but when I got up from my chair and reached for my wallet, he rose quickly. He was reacting as if I was about to pull a weapon. He said, "We cannot take your money here. You must go back to Kyiv and pay at a bank there."

This wasn't the first time I had been required to pay government funds to a bank. The tourist visa application fee I had paid had to be taken to the bank. The government officials in Ukraine were so corrupt they didn't trust any of them with money. The bank procedure was designed to reduce that corruption. I knew I had already missed my flight, so that pressure was off, but going back to Kyiv to pay a fine meant it was likely going to be the next day before I could leave the country. In the grand scheme of things, this wasn't a big deal, but I couldn't wait to get the hell out of Ukraine.

The border officer told me to stay in the room. He went out for ten minutes. When he returned, he told me he had been given authority to allow me to sign a voucher and pay the fine to a U.S. bank. The woman at the desk quickly typed the voucher. I signed it immediately. He then told me, "If you fail to pay the fine in the U.S., you will be barred from Ukraine forever." I was thinking I didn't give a flying fuck about coming back, until I realized my fiancé lived here.

When I had signed the voucher, the officer told me I was free to go. I hit the door and went directly to the front of the line at customs. I thought there was a chance my flight might be delayed because of the weather. The people in line were complaining and I was apologizing, but I had to get out of there.

The border officer stamped my passport, and I ran toward my gate. It was a long way and I suddenly realized there was no moisture in my mouth. It was a very strange feeling. I wasn't that thirsty but there was no saliva in my mouth. I later realized it was nerves. I had never been that nervous in my life.

When I got to my gate, there was a large crowd lined up to talk to the airline agent. I couldn't understand much of it, but I could tell the flight had been delayed. Finally, someone asked how long it would be before the plane boarded and I heard the agent say at least an hour. I had never been so happy about a delayed flight in my life.

I sat down and did an internet search on the time a foreign citizen could stay in Ukraine without a visa.

I had done this before, but I must have missed something. I hadn't missed anything. It was clear that I could stay in the country for up to 90 days in any 180 days. I read the rule again to make sure. I also messaged Oksana and told her about my border ordeal. She told me she was at the train station, but she was coming back to the airport to make sure I had no further problems. Bless her little heart. This was another notice I should have filed in my brain. *You don't leave anyone alone in a foreign country.* I told her to stay at the train station and that I would keep her posted.

Then, I did something that most people will have a hard time believing. I decided to go back and try to explain that I had done nothing illegal. It had nothing to do with the fine. It had everything to do with my fiancé living in Ukraine.

When I returned to the border gates, all of the big red arrows were pointing toward me. You could come out of the country this way, but you could not reenter the country. None of the regular gates were being used. I walked down to where the pilots and crews were coming through a special gate. I asked one of the pilots if he spoke English. He said yes. I told him I had a legal border issue and I needed to talk with a border officer. He told me to wait, and he would get someone. In less than two minutes he returned. Walking beside him was the same officer who had interrogated me!

He said, "It's you again. What you want?" I told him my fiancé lived in Ukraine and I couldn't risk not being able to come back. He told me to follow him. I couldn't believe I had put myself back into a trap from which I had so recently escaped, but that decision was made, and it was too late to change my mind.

We went back to the same small room. He sat down. He didn't invite me to sit. He took out a piece of paper and drew a horizontal line. He was pressing the pencil so hard on the paper that the graphite was flying. He told me, "I am going to explain this to you one more time. Listen carefully." He put a zero on one end of the horizontal line and 180 on the other end. He then put 90 in the middle. He pointed to the 90, and said, "You are only allowed to stay *nineteen* days in each 180 days." Son of a bitch! I had broken the foreign code. He was saying *nineteen*, but he meant *ninety*. One small word had been the total cause of our misunderstanding.

I knew I had not stayed more than ninety days in Ukraine. There was absolutely no doubt. I looked at my passport again. It was quickly clear to me what had happened. The passport was stamped when you entered the country and again when you left the country. On one of my trips, the date stamp had hit my passport at an angle and there was no way to read the date I had left the country. So they just assumed I hadn't left the country. I tried to explain to the officer what had happened. I thought he understood.

The border officer told me to wait in the room again. I had no idea where he was going, how long he might be gone, or what he was doing. Fortunately, my passport was scanned into the computer immigration system in addition to it being stamped. When he checked the system, he determined that I had, indeed, been in his country for less than ninety days.

When he returned to the small room, he told me I was free to go. Hell, I felt certain I was free to go. I had just gone and come back! I asked if I was going to have any issues when I came back to Ukraine. He said, "You are welcome to come back to Ukraine anytime." Then I took the voucher out of my pocket and asked him if I should pay the fine. I just wanted to make certain I didn't get screwed by the computer system. He took the voucher out of my hand, tore it in half, and threw it in the trash. He turned and left. There was no apology, no handshake, and no goodbye kiss.

I went back through Ukraine customs for the third time in an hour. I walked to my gate. I called Oksana and told her everything was finally good, and I was leaving in a few minutes. She said, for the one-hundredth time, "Welcome to Ukraine!"

Visas

Chapter Eighty-Three

On January 1, I had begun giving Oksana a $500 monthly allowance. She didn't ask for the money, but we were engaged to be married and I wanted her to be comfortable in Kharkiv. She told me the amount was more than enough for her monthly expenses. It isn't much money in the U.S., but it made a big difference in Ukraine.

We had decided we didn't want to be apart for more than four weeks at any one time until the visa was approved. So, we began to plan our next meeting immediately. I got on the internet and discovered that Oksana could travel from Ukraine to Mexico and the visa application process there was very simple. Cancun was a great Mexican tourist area, and it was a short flight from Birmingham.

It took Oksana five minutes online to get a Mexican visa! It's called an eectronic authorization and it's good for up to 180 days. I went to Hotels.com and booked us a room at The Royal Caribbean on the beach in Cancun. However, when I began checking on flights from Ukraine to Cancun, I ran into some serious issues. Mexico might have been excited to get visitors, but most countries would not even allow Oksana to land at their airport to change planes.

When I searched the available flights most of them went through Atlanta, but she couldn't even change planes in Atlanta without what is called a transit visa. I didn't know how difficult these were to obtain and I wasn't interested in finding out if there was any other way to get her to Mexico.

I began to make calls to various airlines and search the internet for countries that would allow her to change planes at their airports. It wasn't extremely clear, but it appeared that France would allow her to use Charles de Gaulle airport. She would not be allowed to leave the airport but that shouldn't have been a problem, so I booked a flight through Paris and booked my flight through Miami, Florida. I arranged for us to arrive on the same day, and I was able to book a flight that would allow me to be at the airport when she arrived.

When I arrived at the Cancun Airport on February 19, around 2,000 people were waiting in line to clear customs. Don't fly to Cancun on a Sunday. Mexico's economy would likely collapse if it lost its tourist revenue. You can easily see this in the Cancun Airport. It is a modern facility that would work well except for the customs area. The waiting room is a huge auditorium. So, they are expecting a large crowd. If this is the case, why didn't they have more customs officers at the gates?

It took two hours to get to the gate and ten seconds to clear customs. Oksana was scheduled to arrive about three hours later, so I had some time to kill and to begin thinking about all of the things that could go wrong. The worst issue was communications. Her cellphone had a Ukraine SIM card, and it wasn't working well internationally. She was able to tell me she had made it to Paris and was about to board her plane to Cancun but that was an eleven-hour flight and that was a long time to be incommunicado. I was beginning to think in Spanish. When she landed in Cancun, we could not communicate. I thought she was somewhere in that sea of people, but I was on one side of the border, and she was on the other.

I recalled that Oksana had borrowed a large suitcase from her brother for the trip. She had taken a picture of it at her flat just before the taxi came to take her to the airport. So, I waited at the luggage carousel. When I finally saw the suitcase, it was the best I had felt in days. I had stopped by the airport liquor store and purchased some good tequila, but that was wearing off.

I walked up and down the Mexican side of the gates for over an hour looking for Oksana in the crowd. When I saw her at one of the gates, she was waving her hands in the air and smiling. She didn't appear to be the least bit worried about anything.

When she cleared customs and walked into Mexico, I kissed her and began to settle down and breathe normally. We took a taxi to the hotel. Cancun had made significant improvements in its highway system since I had been there and the drive to the hotel was lovely. Oksana liked Mexico immediately and we were happy to be together again.

Chapter Eighty-Four

The Royal Caribbean wasn't the finest hotel on the beach in Cancun, but it wasn't not the most expensive either. When you are planning an extended stay, a few hundred dollars a night adds up quickly. I thought the room was adequate and there were a lot of activities available. The beach was beautiful and there were several restaurants on the property. Several of the restaurants were good and one was terrible. I just couldn't eat the food they served. The rest of the food in Mexico was good. A couple of restaurants were exceptional.

We had a good time at The Royal Caribbean. We played water volleyball, did the pool exercise program, sat by the pool, and walked along the beach. Oksana bought a large white hat at the hotel, and she wore it during our entire five-week stay in Mexico. I must have taken a hundred pictures of her in that hat. She was beautiful.

On February 21, we rented a car and drove down to Playa del Carmen. I hadn't been there in years, and I wanted to see if it had changed. It was hard to believe how many people were there. My daughter and I had been on a scuba diving trip twenty years before and it was just a small village.

Now the main street was closed to cars, and it was packed with people. We found a small café and ate some good Mexican food and drank a couple of beers. After lunch, we walked around for a while before heading back to Cancun. Oksana wanted to drive the rental car. I was a little nervous about it because I knew she would try anything, but she did fine. She was a good driver. The traffic was terrible because of highway construction but she handled it well. Of course, she said, "Photo please."

The big white hat

We would have stayed at The Royal Caribbean, but when our booking was over, they had no rooms available. I got on Airbnb and found us an apartment on the beach in an area known as Playa del Mar. We took a taxi to look at the property and decided to take it. We moved in on February 24.

The apartment was located in a beachfront resort away from the hotel district. The resort consisted of three high-rise buildings with gardens, a restaurant, and a huge pool between the buildings, and the beach.

The owner of the apartment was a nice guy by the name of Mahatma. He spoke only Spanish, but he was always fair and did everything he said he would do.

When Mahatma was showing use around, Oksana saw an iguana and completely lost it. She ran screaming in the opposite direction. It was as if she had seen a tyrannosaurus. It didn't seem to register with her that the kids playing everywhere didn't appear to be in any danger. I had seen the animals before and I knew they were not aggressive, but Oksana had never seen anything like them, and she was mortified. These animals were up to four feet long and I understood Oksana's initial fear. Mahatma just smiled and said, "She will be playing with them before you leave here."

There was a good restaurant near the beach and the pool. The gym was also in that area, but you had to run the iguana gauntlet to reach it. For the first few days, Oksana wouldn't go anywhere near the animals. I took the handle off a mop that was in the apartment and gave it to her. This gave her a sense of security and she soon overcame her fear. We called the mop handle the iguana stick.

Oksana and her "Iguana Stick"

I took several pictures of Oksana teasing the iguana. She had learned they weren't aggressive, and she was now having fun with them. My theory is anything with teeth can bite and an iguana has teeth. So I didn't mess with them and they never bothered me. I am a little surprised they didn't bite Oksana.

I'm not photogenic, but one of the pictures we had someone take of us together was very good and I suggested she replace her Viber photo with it. I was surprised when she vigorously objected. She told me there were people she didn't want to know about us. I couldn't believe she felt that way and certainly didn't understand why she told me.

We disagreed and she contacted her witch about it. Her witch told her I was wrong not to understand that a woman needs her independence. This didn't sound like traditional values to me. I didn't give a damn what her witch had said. If I had one, I would expect her to agree with me. But I did care about her decision regarding the photo. It was another huge red flag and I was beginning to see them more clearly.

Chapter Eighty-Five

We were together for just over five weeks in Cancun. I went to Birmingham one time for three days to take care of my income tax returns and some other financial matters. Oksana wasn't happy about my leaving, but I had told her about it in advance and she didn't complain too much.

Our days at Playa del Mar were a combination of sunning by the pool, working out at the gym, grilling in the resort gardens, eating at various restaurants, shopping for groceries, and going on some excursions. It was a very relaxing time for us, but Oksana was a very active woman and she wanted to be doing something different just about every day. I could remember being the same way when I was younger. This was an issue, but I didn't think it was a big problem. It did, however, remind me of our age difference.

The restaurant on the property was a large thatched-roof building near the pool. The food wasn't great, but we liked the staff and we soon learned what to order. Most of the time we ate at one of the dozen or so tables inside the open-air building but sometimes we asked them to serve our food by the pool. The menu was a combination of Mexican and American items, and the prices were very reasonable.

We almost always ate breakfast in our apartment. I would often prepare an omelet for Oksana, and I would have my usual cereal and coffee. This was before I learned that cereal is one of the worst foods you can eat. It is extremely high in sugar and other carbohydrates, and sugar was poison. In the evenings, we usually went to a little restaurant just down the beach from the hotel called Puerto Santos. The food there was superb. The seafood came off the fishing boats docked nearby. When you ordered fish, they brought out several whole raw fish on a platter, you could pick the one you wanted, and they would prepare it any way you liked. There were fish of all sizes. Some were for one person, and some were large enough for a table of people. It was some of the best seafood I had ever had. The fish was served with the head on, and it was delicious.

There was a guacamole cart at Puerto Santos. You could pick the ingredients you liked, and the lady would make your dish at the table. In addition to the usual avocado, cilantro, onion, tomatoes, and lime juice, many other ingredients could be added to suit your taste. My Spanish wasn't good, and we had a little trouble communicating with the wait staff.

One evening our regular waiter who spoke English asked me if I wanted to add a little crunch to my guacamole and showed me some small dark brown pieces of something that I thought were roasted peppers. I ask the waiter if they were hot and told me they were not. The lady added the crunchy item, and the result was delicious. The texture was distinctly different, and the taste was better. Later, when I walked by the guacamole cart, I could see this crunchy ingredient better in the light by the bar. It wasn't roasted pepper. It was roasted crickets.

We were regulars at Puerto Santos. The place was almost always busy and there was often live music. There was a nice bar in the rear and the restaurant tables spilled out toward the beach on one side. It was a perfect setting. You couldn't possibly get fresher seafood and the prices were about half of what you would expect to pay in the States. The owner was a handsome young Mexican man of about 40. He often came to our table and thanked us for coming. It was a nice touch. This guy knew how to run a restaurant.

I checked a popular website and found a couple of restaurants nearby that looked good. The ratings were excellent, so we decided to give them a try. The first one was a fifteen-minute walk from the resort. It was a small open-air restaurant with a grill out front on the sidewalk. The smell of grilled fish filled the air. There were a couple of seats vacant at the bar, but we chose a small table near the wall. I think we were the only tourists in the place.

I ordered the ceviche, which is a very popular raw seafood salad and Oksana picked the grilled octopus. I was a little surprised at her selection because she is usually a very conservative eater. When the octopus came to the table there was no mistaking what it was. This wasn't grilled octopus parts; it was the whole sea creature. The meal was wonderful. I ate some of the octopus, but Oksana declined my offer of raw fish.

When we didn't go out to eat, we grilled at the resort. There were two grilling areas in the gardens. There was a grill and a couple of tables in each area. The place was kept immaculately clean. All you needed was some charcoal and your food and wine. It was a lot of fun and we did it often. Oksana loved grilled meat and vegetables. She would make this moaning sound when she was eating the meal. On one occasion I took a picture of her licking her plate. I think she was just showing me she liked what I had prepared. More than likely it was simply Oksana creating another photo opportunity.

The landscaping at Playa del Mar was elaborate and fast-growing in the Mexican climate. There were always people working in the gardens. One afternoon I asked one of the guys trimming the shrubs if he could climb up one of the many coconut palm trees and get Oksana a fresh coconut. It took him about one minute to climb the tree and throw a huge coconut to the ground. He took his machete and cut the top off and we took the coconut to the restaurant. I asked the waiter to pour some rum and Grand Marnier into the fresh coconut and bring us two straws. It was a real treat.

Almost every day we spent some time at the pool. There were a surprising number of Russian-speaking people at the resort. I assumed it was because the visa process was automatic. Oksana became friends with a young Ukrainian woman who had met a Mexican man on a dating site. They had been married a few years and she had her two-year-old daughter with her. The woman was about 27 years old and beautiful. She was thin and had long dark blonde hair. Her daughter had jet black hair and none of her mother's features. A few days later, when the woman's husband came to the pool, it was obvious where their daughter got most of her DNA.

Chapter Eighty-Six

I didn't relax much during my working career. I worked. When I joined the highway construction company where I spent 27 years, annual sales were around $6 million. When I retired, we had made 49 acquisitions and annual sales had grown to about $150 million. Acquiring businesses and integrating them into the organization was a difficult and time-consuming job.

Every time I was away from work, I felt like I should be back minding the store and that didn't make for great vacations. I understood I wasn't that critical to the business, and it was my problem, but I just never was able to solve it.

After I retired, I was finally able to completely relax. I thought the relaxing lifestyle at the resort was ideal. Oksana seemed to be happy, but she was often suggesting other more exciting activities. One of those activities was snorkeling.

Isla Mujeres is an island just east of Playa del Mar. The ferry to the island was a ten-minute walk from our apartment. Several snorkeling tours were available at the dock from which the ferry leaves. We picked one and took the next boat. Oksana loved the wind in her hair on the ride to the island. It was a lovely day, and the temperature was perfect. A young man was singing Mexican songs and the Corona was cold.

Our tour guide and boat captain met us at the dock and led us to his small boat. There were eight or ten other people already on the boat. We sat down and were soon headed along the shore on our way to a dive reef. When we arrived at the reef, we were given some abbreviated instructions and then dumped into the water. Not much could go wrong because we were required to wear a life preserver while in the water. This, of course, wasn't snorkeling because you couldn't dive, but it was safe.

I had bought us masks and snorkels and Oksana had learned to use them in the resort pool. At first, she had a difficult time clearing the water from the tube when she came to the surface. Water enters the snorkel when you go under, and the first thing that must be done when you surface is forcefully blow the water out of the tube. If you don't do this the first thing into your lungs will be water instead of air. When that water is salty, it isn't a pleasant experience. It can also cause panic and that can create a very dangerous situation very quickly. This is one of the first lessons you learn in scuba training.

This wasn't much of an issue while we were "snorkeling" at Isla Mujeres because the life preservers kept us on the surface. Oksana did very well, and she was having a good time looking at the fish and coral. The fish were very colorful at shallow depths, and it was by far the best way to view them. At a hundred feet with scuba gear on, what you see is mostly gray. I believe ninety percent of scuba divers should stay within thirty-five feet of the surface. The colors are vivid and if you have a problem, you simply discard your equipment and swim to the surface. At a hundred feet, it takes several minutes to reach the surface to avoid the bends.

The captain picked us up and we were moving to another reef when Oksana got seasick. She didn't get in the water at the next reef, and she wasn't feeling well at all. I have never been seasick, but I am told it is awful. Later when we stopped along the shore for lunch, we walked down the beach to a somewhat deserted area and Oksana threw up. She only vomited the water she had been drinking but she felt a little better immediately. I was surprised when she was able to eat some lunch, but after that, she was much better and was ready to go.

We had a good time on the tour, but Oksana didn't ask to do any more snorkeling or boat riding. That little episode of seasickness was enough for her. And snorkeling with a life preserver holding you on the surface wasn't that much fun anyway.

Chapter Eighty-Seven

We booked a bus tour to the Mayan ruins at Chichen Itza for March 16. We met the tour bus at the ferry dock. It was a three- hour drive from the dock. On the way to Chichen Itza, we stopped at a small Mayan village. The people were poor, and the tour operators made these stops to help them earn a meager living. They sell trinkets and silver jewelry. There was also a restaurant there where we ate lunch.

The tour guide on the bus had told us about some Mayan calendars the people in the village printed on old paper. You gave them some personal information and they custom made the calendar to fit the data. It was supposed to have some magical properties and Oksana appeared to believe it. She filled out the little form and gave it to me.

At the village, I bought her a silver pendant with her name on it in the Mayan language. It took about an hour for the pendant to be made, but we were about to eat lunch there, so it wasn't a problem. After we purchased a few more items, we walked over to where a Mayan priest was trying to sell blessings. The magic held within the items we bought could only be released if each item was blessed by the priest. I knew it was bullshit, but Oksana didn't want to take any chances just in case he was right. So, I paid $20 for the blessing ceremony.

Oksana sat on a small stool and the priest walked around her and sprinkled water on her head. He then took a smoking bundle of twigs and leaves and danced around her several times. After about five minutes the items we had bought were loaded with magical powers. Oksana was so excited.

We ate a good Mexican buffet and then went back to pick up her pendant. They had done a nice job and she liked the results. We were finished and were about to get on the bus when I discovered I had forgotten to give Oksana's personal information to the woman who made the Mayan calendars. When I told her about this, she went ballistic. She started screaming at me in Russian just as we were getting on the bus. Neither I nor the people on the bus knew what she was saying, but everyone knew she was as mad as hell. I had likely fucked up her magic for years. That little episode set the tone for the rest of the day. She was upset about the magic, and I was upset because I had asked her many times not to wash our dirty linen in public.

Chichen Itza was a remarkable place for a lot of reasons. It was privately owned, and it had to be making the owner a fortune. There must have been a thousand visitors there that day. The Mayans were interesting people. They were very intelligent and even more religious—which seemed somewhat contradictory to me.

One of the most bizarre things I learned had to do with a game the Mayans played on a large court that resembled a football field. There was a stone ring about twenty feet off the ground. The hole in the stone appeared to be about a foot in diameter. The first team to put the ball through the hole won the match. I don't know the rules of the game.

The game wasn't bizarre—the prize for the captain of the winning team was. The captain of the winning team had the honor of being sacrificed to the gods in a pit of water about a hundred yards from the stadium. The pit is still there today. A stone was tied to his body, and he was ceremoniously pushed into the pit. I am told it was a great and glorious day for the entire family. This sounds incredible until you think about modern-day suicide bombers. At least the Mayan captain didn't insist on taking a group of spectators with him.

The other remarkable thing about Chichen Itza was the incredible about of Chichen shit trinkets for sale everywhere. There must have been 200 vendors there selling the cheapest trash I had ever seen. Fortunately, Oksana didn't insist on purchasing anything. I don't think I could have forced myself to do it.

On the way back to Cancun the bus stopped in a small town so we could all spend some more dollars in Mexico. I bought Oksana a silver chain to go with her Mayan pendant. We were in love again. The trip lasted thirteen hours. That was too long to keep my undivided attention. When we returned to the apartment, I was exhausted. I have visited my last Mayan ruin.

Chapter Eighty-Eight

Sex with Oksana was always good. I haven't mentioned sex much here because something was happening in Mexico that made it different there. For some reason, she was not as happy as she had always been in Ukraine. There were some issues and misunderstandings as I had mentioned, but during those last few days in Cancun, there seemed to be something else going on that was affecting the passionate component of our relationship.

On the night of March 23, we went to Puerto Santos for dinner. It was later than usual and there weren't many people eating. We had a great meal and drank some good Pinot Grigio. As we were leaving, Oksana noticed a hammock in the yard beside the restaurant. She ran and jumped into the hammock. She immediately began asking me to take her photo. The light wasn't good, it was late, and I wanted to go to the apartment. But I took a couple of pictures with my cellphone. That was not enough. She continued to say, "Photo, please. Photo, please." I was beginning to think she was demanding these pictures to test my obedience, but that could easily be paranoia. I finally told her I was going to the apartment. She said she was staying.

I walked down the beach toward the Playa del Mar. It was late at night and there was almost no one around. There was some activity in the boats at the dock, but I couldn't see what was going on. When I got back to the entrance to the resort, I stopped and sat on a bench that was there by the gate. There was also a guard at the gate. I sat there for about fifteen minutes and began to worry about leaving Oksana in the hammock. I decided to go back for her. I thought my returning for her would make everything all right between us. I was wrong.

When I asked her to come with me, she said she wanted to stay there and think. She told me to go without her. That was not an option. This was Mexico. The U.S. State Department had recently issued a warning about kidnapping in the country. Oksana was my responsibility. She had had too much to drink. I took her by the hand. She resisted. I physically pulled her out of the hammock and forced her toward the beach. She finally stopped resisting and we returned to the apartment. She immediately noticed she had lost a part of her shoe during the ordeal at the restaurant. She wanted me to go back and look for the lost part. It was midnight and I refused. She told me she expected me to replace her damaged shoes.

That was not a good night for us. I was up with the sun the next morning. I drank a cup of coffee and headed to Puerto Santos to look for the shoe part. When I got to the restaurant there were four or five young guys hanging around the place. I don't know what they were doing there, but they were friendly and asked me what I was looking for. We worked out the language issue and soon they were helping me look for the missing shoe part. We combed the area. We found some weird items, but not the shoe ornament. On the way back to the apartment, I searched along the beach. It was the proverbial needle in the haystack.

I stopped by the resort restaurant and ate breakfast. I was in no hurry to deliver the bad news to Oksana. I still loved her, but I sensed she was slipping away.

Chapter Eighty-Nine

How can so great a love dies? It is impossible to answer the question. Maybe the love wasn't ever that great. Maybe there was one fatal mistake. Maybe it was death by a thousand cuts. What does it matter? Love might not last forever but death by any means almost certainly does. And our relationship's vital signs were not looking good.

At 6:00 in the evening on March 25, Oksana and I decided to have an early dinner at Puerto Santos. As we were walking through the gardens on a narrow sidewalk, we met a couple walking toward us. There wasn't room for us to pass so I nudged Oksana ahead of me to allow the couple to pass to our left. I could have easily stepped in front of her, but I was putting her in front. When the couple had passed, she shouted at me, "Don't ever push me again!" I explained that I was just moving her ahead of me to allow the couple to pass. She was angry and repeated, "No! You pushed me!"

She began to shove me off the sidewalk. She told me that was how I had been shoving her. I didn't understand because there was no way I was pushing her off the sidewalk. It just did not happen.

We continued our walk to Puerto Santos. The weather was perfect, so we chose an outside table. The food was simply incredible. The owner came out and thanked us for coming. Oksana was lovely. I took my camera out of my pocket to take a picture. She immediately said, "No photo." I had never heard those words come out of her mouth. I was shocked. Something was really wrong.

Finally, Oksana told me she was depressed. She quickly added she wanted to go home to Ukraine and think about everything. I reminded her we were engaged to be married. She said, "I love you, but I need some time to think." She told me she didn't think it would take her long to make her decision. I wondered how she could know this.

Incredibly, Oksana told me she wanted us to stay together in Cancun for the twelve days left on our apartment lease. I could not imagine how we could stay together in Cancun when I knew she was going back home to make a decision about the rest of our lives. I vividly imagined the Sword of Damocles hanging over my head for twelve days. I didn't think there was a chance I could put myself in that position. I asked for the check, and we walked back to Puerto del Mar.

The next morning, I asked Oksana if she wanted to go home immediately. She told me again she would prefer to stay with me in Cancun for the next couple of weeks. I told her I wanted her to go home as soon as possible so the clock could start on her decision. I tried to tell her the reason I couldn't stay in Cancun when she wasn't sure about us. She said she didn't understand.

But we soon agreed to leave Cancun as soon as reasonably possible. Changing booked non-refundable airline reservations is difficult and expensive. This is one of the most effective ways airline companies make their money. They know plans change and they are ready to fuck you when that happens. I am not in favor of government control of anything, but I might listen to an argument for more regulation of the airline industry.

The options for Oksana's return flight to Ukraine were limited. Again, we were faced with the issue of finding an airport where she could change planes. After hours of research, calls, and emails, we determined she could possibly return through Frankfurt, Germany. The change to Condor Airlines would cost about $600.

Before I changed her flight, I once again asked Oksana if this was what she wanted to do. She was upset about the situation, but she agreed going home early was the best choice, so she told me to book the flight.

Before we decided to go to Mexico for the extended stay, we had agreed I would return to Birmingham for two short visits. The return flight for the second visit was booked weeks before and that flight was scheduled to depart Cancun two days before Oksana's revised departure. I had a choice. I could change my flight, or Oksana would be in Mexico for two days without me. The cost of the change was more than the original round-trip ticket. Oksana had her new friend in Mexico and the owner of the apartment was available to assist her if needed. She would also be in constant communication with me on Viber. The only argument for staying was I would be at the airport to put Oksana on the plane and say goodbye to her there. That didn't seem all that important to me but later I discovered it was hugely important to Oksana.

My plane departed early, and Oksana was in bed until I was ready to walk out the apartment door. She got out of bed to kiss me goodbye. It only lasted a couple of minutes. I said, "Goodbye, Oksy." I felt reasonably certain I would never see her again. The taxi was waiting to take me to the airport. I turned to leave, and I didn't look back.

Chapter Ninety

After I left Cancun, Oksana went berserk. She accused me of leaving her stranded in a strange land. She said a real man would have reached out to her and comforted her when she was depressed and homesick. Her accusations hit home. I felt guilty and ashamed. She had told me she was going home to think about us. Was she actually reaching out to me for support or was her mind made up about us? I will never know for sure.

At the time, she told me she was uncertain about us; I went into heart preservation mode. I didn't feel like reaching out and comforting. And deep down inside, I was thinking all of her lies had come home to roost. She was finally telling the truth.

Oksana discussed what had happened with her witch and with her Mexican friend. They both agreed I was not a real man. The Mexican friend's husband even told Oksana that only a faggot would leave his fiancé in a foreign country alone. I might not have handled the situation correctly, but I didn't see how that affected my sexual orientation. I guess he was just trying to call me the worst name he could think of with his limited vocabulary. Honestly, I didn't give a damn.

Oksana settled down long enough to ask me to send her some money for the return trip to Ukraine. I sent her the money and arranged for her to have a window seat and a premium meal on her flight to Frankfort. I stayed online 24 hours a day in case she needed to contact me for any reason. I was feeling guilty, and she knew it.

Our K1-visa was approved one week from the day Oksana left Mexico. I sent her a picture of the notice. We communicated on Viber for a few days after she got home. She finally told me she wanted to stay in Ukraine. She said she was ending the engagement. I knew it was the right decision for both of us, but I also knew it was going to be a difficult road to travel for a long time.

About a month after we left Mexico, I asked Oksana if she wanted to meet in Kyiv and try to work out our issues. She told me it would be a waste of time and money. That was about as clear as it got. Sometimes I wish my father had been a little clearer when he told me, "Son, you traded for it," but I think I'm beginning to understand it better. Love is a great teacher if you can survive the lesson.

Even after she ended the relationship, Oksana couldn't help asking for my help. In one of her last Viber messages, she launched into an upcoming trip to Egypt with her friend Tanya. She talked about how she needed to get away and think. She told me she would likely not be able to go because she didn't have any money. Then she told me exactly how much money she needed, in U.S. dollars, for the trip. It was obvious she was asking me for the money. I thought this was callused and insensitive. She didn't want me, but she was addicted to my money. I didn't even reply to her message.

Oksana had my mailing address in Birmingham, but I sent it to her on Viber anyway. I asked her to send me the two engagement rings. She told me it was a

Ukrainian custom to keep the rings if the engagement was broken off. I hope that is the last lie I ever hear from Oksana.

Chapter Ninety-One

Some of my close friends predicted I would be over Oksana in a week. They had warned me of the coming disaster long before I faced the facts. They thought that once I saw the truth, it would be easy to move on. They didn't know the depths of my feelings and they didn't understand the extent of my blindness. It took a few weeks to begin to feel like I was making much progress. Finally, the bottoms weren't as low, and I was returning to normal activities. Healing was going to be a long process, but I could tell I was making incremental progress.

There was, however, one issue I couldn't shake. I couldn't get Oksana's parents off my mind. A commitment is serious business, and the one I had made just a few weeks earlier at the Opera Hotel was fresh on my mind. A man is no better than his word. I had made solemn promises and just couldn't deal with someone thinking I had lied to them.

I wrestled with the issue for several weeks. Finally, I decided to write a letter to Oksana's father. I had his address from the K1-visa application. The letter had a single purpose. I had made a promise to him, and I wanted him to know I would have kept that promise if it had been possible.

Уважаемый Миколай,

Я знаю, что вы не ожидаете получить это письмо. Я не собирался писать. Но я никогда не оставлял нерешенные вопросы.

Теперь я уверен, что Оксана сказала вам, что наша помолвка закончилась. Она, без сомнения, рассказала вам, как я покинул ее в Мексике. Она сказала мне, и другие, я не настоящий мужчина, и я не заслуживаю настоящей женщины. Это то, что люди говорят о человеке, которого они когда-то любили. Я полностью понимаю.

Я пишу вам это письмо, потому что я обещал вам и матерью Оксаны в Киеве, что я никогда не причиню вреда вашей дочери. Я сказал тебе, что я тоже отец, и я понял твою заботу о твоей дочери. Я видел слезы в твоих глазах. Я был глубоко тронут.

Я не понимаю, что произошло в Мексике. Однажды вечером мы обедали, и Оксана сказала, что она тосковала по родине и хотела вернуться домой и подумать о наших отношениях. Я был потрясен и удивлен. Она сказала, что хотела быть со мной в Мексике в течение оставшихся двенадцати дней нашего пребывания, но я просто не мог этого сделать. Я был разбит сердцем. Я попросил ее вернуться в Украину и принять ее решение. Теперь я полагаю, что ее решение уже было принято. У Оксаны есть секретная жизнь, и некоторые из них она ни с кем не делится.

Я сделал все возможное, чтобы устроить отъезд из Мексики. Изменение рейсов было чрезвычайно затруднительным, поскольку большинство стран не позволяло Оксане сменить самолеты в своих аэропортах.

Моя единственная цель написать это письмо - сказать вам, что я не делаю обещаний, которые я не намерен хранить. Я имел в виду каждое обещание, которое я сделал вам в Киеве. Я любил твою дочь, и я хотел жениться на ней и заботиться о ней всю оставшуюся жизнь. Она приняла решение прекратить отношения.

Надеюсь, это письмо ответит на некоторые из вопросов, которые могут возникнуть в конце нашего участия. Я желаю вам всего наилучшего, Оксана и остальная часть вашей семьи.

С уважением

For those who don't read Russian, here is the English translation:

Dear Mykolai,
I know you are not expecting to receive this letter. I was not expecting to write it, but I have never been one to leave outstanding issues unresolved.
By now, I am sure Oksana has told you our engagement has ended. She has, no doubt, told you how I deserted her in Mexico. She told me, and others, I am not a real man and I don't deserve a real woman. These are the things people say about the person they once loved. I completely understand. I am writing you this letter because I made a promise to you and Oksana's mother in Kyiv that I would never hurt

your daughter in any way. I told you I was also a father and I understood your concern for your daughter. I saw the tears in your eyes. I was deeply moved.

I don't understand what happened in Mexico. One night we were having dinner and Oksana told me she was homesick and wanted to go home and think about our relationship. I was shocked and surprised. She said she wanted to be with me in Mexico for the remaining twelve days of our stay, but I just could not do that. I was heartbroken. I asked her to return to Ukraine and make her decision. I now believe her decision was already made. Oksana has a secret life and some of it she shares with no one.

I did my very best to arrange our departure from Mexico. Changing the flights was extremely difficult since most countries would not allow Oksana to change planes at their airports.

My only purpose of writing this letter is to tell you I don't make promises I don't intend to keep. I meant every promise I made to you in Kyiv. I loved your daughter and I wanted to marry her and take care of her for the rest of her life. She decided to end the relationship.

I hope this letter answers some of the questions you may have about the ending of our engagement. I wish only the very best for you, Oksana, and the rest of your family.
Sincerely,

Chapter Ninety-Two

The original purpose of telling this story was to help me understand what had happened. Then I began to think it might help others avoid the critical mistakes I had made. After the story was virtually told, I wanted to examine the results and try to determine if at least some of this had been accomplished. I tried to take an objective look at the important elements. I wanted to determine how this was possible and to learn from the experience.

There is no doubt in my mind Oksana was working for Ukraine Brides and talking to many men at the same time. She told me several times she was only talking to me. Of course, she also told Ken she wasn't interested in other men.

Recovery from love–blindness is a slow process. When I began to tell the story about the massive letter-writing campaign, it never occurred to me Ukraine Brides was writing most of Oksana's letters. Even when there were duplicate letters, I attributed them to Oksana. The entire process was orchestrated by the site. The woman does little more than provide smiling pictures and embellishes the letters with personal comments. The mistakes in the names are mistakes by the site. They just can't keep all of their clients straight.

Oksana constantly demanded photographs of herself to provide a bank of pictures to post on dating sites. There is no doubt in my mind that if I were to go on any number of the many Russian dating sites, I would find pictures of Oksana I took in Ukraine and

Mexico. I don't have the stomach for that search, but I am virtually certain of the results.

Oksana had worked for a bank for some period during the past several years, but she no longer worked there. She was officially unemployed on the public record. I couldn't imagine a bank allowing an employee to take off for sixty days in one year. She was likely telling her family the same lie she was telling me about her employment.

Oksana's desire for me to meet her parents was more difficult to understand. When it was happening, I narrowed the reasons down to two. Either the relationship was real, or her parents were in on the scam. After I spent three days with her mother and father, I was convinced they were genuine, honest people. That forced me to conclude the relationship was real. However, with the benefit of hindsight, I have discovered a third possibility. I believe it explains Oksana involving her parents in our relationship.

As incredible as it sounds, when a woman in Ukraine reaches the age of forty, she is considered an old maid. She will likely never get a husband. She will never have children and she will never provide grandchildren for her parents. Something was wrong with her. The powerful driving force of family tradition had its downside. The pressure could be relentless.

I believe this pressure on Oksana became unbearable, so she decided to arrange a dog and pony show starring a real American man. She asked her parents to travel a great distance to attend this production. She did a masterful job and completely sold them.

The problem was that she oversold them. Her parents loved me. They never questioned my love for their daughter. Her mother even told Oksana at the engagement ceremony she better never hurt me.

During our last few days in Mexico, I noticed Oksana was preoccupied. When she told me about her homesickness, I attributed her preoccupation to the distress caused by that issue. After it was all over, I began to see the bigger picture.

She had begun to do little things that would upset me. It was almost like she was trying to make me angry and start an argument. For example, the pushing incident just before our last supper had been inexplicable. When her verbal assault didn't get the desired results, she began physically shoving me off the sidewalk. She had made up her mind she was going home, but she was having trouble finding an excuse.

That's when Oksana got lucky. She had agreed to return to Ukraine early and she knew how difficult it was going to be to coordinate our departure. Only a couple of countries would allow her to land at their airports. It became a logistical nightmare. It would have been virtually impossible to arrange our flights from Cancun on the same day.

When I left two days early, it was an answer to her prayers. I instantly became the bad guy, and she immediately began to tell everyone who would listen. I am certain this included her family. She had no intention of coming to America. The visa was only days from approval. Her time was running out. My "abandoning" her in Mexico was a godsend for her.

Did Oksana love me? That is an interesting question which makes little difference in the long run. As I have stated, her decision was good for both of us. I should have made the same decision many times. If all this had happened after she came to the U.S., it would have been an emotional and legal nightmare. If she had simply told me the real reason for her decision, it would have been a lot easier for both of us. But some people will lie even when the truth works better. It is inexplicable but true.

Oksana didn't love me in the beginning, and she didn't love me in the end. But in my opinion, there was a period sandwiched in between that she did love me. I think for a little while she sold herself on the idea of giving up her country, her family, her friends, and her lifestyle for life with me in America. Life in Ukraine could be difficult. The economy was in trouble, the politicians were corrupt, the future was bleak, and there was that little issue with Russian bombs and bullets.

Mexico changed Oksana's mind. She did get homesick. She did miss her family and friends. There might have been someone else she missed. I will never know. It doesn't matter. What does matter is the way she orchestrated the final scene. It could have been handled so much better. But for someone who had practiced deception for so long, their go-to position was drama, even when the simple truth would have worked much better for all those involved.

Am I right about all of this? That's not likely. But I am right about most of it. There is a principle of logic known as Occam's Razor. Loosely defined, it states the simplest answer is usually the correct answer. The answers I have given aren't the simplest. They might violate Occam's Razor, but Oksana was not a simple person. Her incredible art of deception had likely made her the exception to the rule.

I had traded for something that, in the end, had little value. Oksana had orchestrated the production, but I had been a willing participant. Almost everyone could see what was happening all along. Oksana was like the Wizard of Oz. My friends had seats where they could see behind the curtain. It must have been excruciating for them to watch me making a fool of myself. They were pointing behind the curtain and telling me what was happening, but they were also trying to maintain our friendship. And not a single one has said I told you so. They likely don't think it's necessary.

A long time after I wrote this chapter, something incredible and unlikely happened that finally answered most of the unresolved issues I was dealing with at that time. When Russia invaded Ukraine, one of the hardest hit cities was Kharkiv, the eastern city where Oksana lives. She had my Viber contact information and she sent me some gruesome photos and videos of the bombings. There was awful destruction and death. Friends were killed and the family business was destroyed. I decided to send some money to Oksana to help her move into the central part of the country to get away from the destruction. I sent the money by Western Union. They required some personal information to ensure accurate delivery of the funds. One required piece of information was Oksana's last name. I noticed Oksana's last name was the name of the man the private detective suspected of living with her. For some reason, I didn't notice the name for months. He was the man Oksana said was a policeman. And he was almost certainly the reason she returned to Ukraine and ended our engagement.

Time is the great healer. If I had learned of this at the time our relationship was ending, I would have been devastated. Of course, when I saw her last name, I was shocked, but I was not destroyed. I didn't even regret sending the money. It was a humanitarian effort to help someone I knew. It may very well have saved Oksana's life.

Seeing that Oksana had married an old lover enabled me to put the final pieces of the complicated puzzle together, and it helped me take the last step away from my Ukraine love affair.

Part Three

*"Memories, may be beautiful and yet
what's too painful to remember
we simply chose to forget.
So it's the laughter we will remember
Whenever we remember
the way we were."*

"Memories" by Mac Davis and Billy Strange

Introduction

The road ahead is more important than the one behind, but the two are inextricably linked.
I love clichés because their truths are so undeniable. There are two that immediately come to mind.
Insanity: Doing the same thing over and over and expecting different results.
And…
Those who cannot remember the past are condemned to repeat it.

As we get older, our life expectancy increases simply because we have survived. We have survived because of our DNA and our ability to make the right decisions most of the time. We decide to not smoke. We decide to work out regularly, to eat a reasonably healthy diet, and to stay away from the edge of both literal and figurative cliffs. We know what helps us live a longer and more productive life, so we chose that lifestyle. Some of that lifestyle isn't much fun but we know it is the best choice.

This doesn't mean we will always make the right choices. For example, I don't have much trouble staying away from literal cliffs. It is much more difficult avoiding the figurative variety.

Chapter Ninety-Three

No one knows the most effective way to deal with a broken heart. Various methods are tried all the time. Country music is full of suggestions. George Jones sang about a man who finally stopped loving a woman; he simply died. Travis Tritt tells us about a failed attempt when he sings, "The Whiskey Ain't Working Anymore." Some people get better results than others with the same methods. For example, Merle Haggard seems to be pleased when he says, "I think I'll Just Sit Here and Drink." I could go on but the examples are limitless, and I think you get the idea.

However, we chose to cope, I don't think sitting alone around the house is a viable option. I understand some people just can't pretend something catastrophic hasn't recently happened. My theory is that life goes on and the sooner we get back to living, the better. This doesn't mean we don't suffer, but I think it accelerates the healing process if we gently force the issue. I have broken a few horses in my life and the simple act of getting back in the saddle comes to mind.

I don't think my father ever had a broken heart. He might have, but, if he did, no one ever knew it. When I broke up with a girl in high school, he told me, "Son, I wouldn't give that girl the pleasure of knowing you are hurting." His philosophy was, "The woods are full of women." I was often in the woods, and I hadn't seen any women out there. I'm only joking, of course.

I think the metaphor he was searching for was that there is plenty of fish in the ocean, but I got his point.

I think you could say my father was a stoic. I saw him hit his thumb with a hammer so hard blood squirted out in several directions. I almost passed out. It affected me more than him. He dealt with emotional issues the very same way. I don't know if he didn't feel the pain or if he was simply internalizing it. Either way, my brother and I didn't inherit this gene. We don't internalize, and we don't try to hide our feelings.

But I am a realist, and I know life goes on after tragedy. So, I soon got up, dusted myself off, and got back to the business of living. For me, that meant finding someone with whom to have dinner and a glass of good white French wine. The healing would take a while, but the process would begin like all journeys—with a single step.

Chapter Ninety-Four

Because the woman to whom I had been engaged had been wearing my ring, I had decided to wear my old wedding ring so other people would know I was committed. It sounds silly in retrospect but people in love often do silly things. When the engagement ended, I immediately removed the ring because I was no longer committed to Oksana, or the general concept of commitment. I was free—for better or worse.

A marriage engagement is a fairly significant event, and some people are devastated when one ends. These people might feel a sense of failure and embarrassment. They don't realize most people have their problems and aren't worried too much about the problems of others. So, I immediately told everyone and then moved on.

I called some of the women I had dated in the past and discovered not much had changed in their lives. It wasn't going to be a problem finding someone to spend time with. Spending time with women is one of my favorite things but the desire to find a long- term relationship just would not leave me alone. It must have been a combination of my age, my decision to not live alone, and my obsessive personality.

Whatever the reasons, I decided to immediately return to the hunt. My first few attempts had failed, but I am not a failure. I knew I had something to contribute to a relationship and I knew we human animals were not meant to be alone. I'm not saying some of us can't be happy living alone; I simply believe most of us want companionship and love.

Chapter Ninety-Five

I was having lunch with one of my dear friends and he mentioned a website that sounded interesting to me. Of course, he knew the details of my recent debacle and he thought he would have a little fun at my expense. When I told him I might be interested, he couldn't believe me. I explained it wasn't internet dating that was inherently bad. It was the flagrant mistakes I had made using it that caused my failures. He still thought I had lost my mind. He knew I had lost my mind. He had been hoping I might have found it somewhere along my recent journey.

The most amazing thing he told me was the name of the website. He said, "You aren't going to believe the name of the dating site; it's Oksanalove.com."

No, it wasn't that Oksana. This Oksana was from Kazakhstan. That country is separated from Ukraine by a southern part of Russia. This Oksana owned a matchmaking business that generally matched Eastern European women with American men. But there was one big difference in her approach to the process. She brought the women to America so the men didn't have to travel to the other side of the world to meet a beautiful woman.

When I had thoroughly researched the website, I decided to give it a try. I talked with Oksana, and I was very impressed. This could be one of those times when the truth sounds unbelievable, but it is vital to the story, and I am going to tell it.

I will not mention Oksana's name any more than necessary because I understand how confusing it can be, and because the name makes me want to throw up. I'll just say she is a smart lady. She had been in business for more than twenty years, and she had been very successful. Many of her clients were happily married. She understood everything about the process. I believe she could successfully run just about any business.

When the women come to the U.S., they would have paid for their visas, their airline tickets, and other travel expenses. The men paid a single payment for attending a four- or five-day meetings with the women. This was not to be confused with an orgy. These women weren't traveling great distances and paying huge prices to meet someone with whom to spend the night. They are all looking for a long-term relationship. Virtually all are looking for marriage.

Most of the women on Oksanalove.com were still in Eastern Europe. They were in the process of obtaining their visas and making their travel arrangements. Some of the women already reside in the U.S. Almost all of them were college graduates and many had advanced degrees. The ages varied widely from young to middle age. This was a lot more like the real world. In every case, these ladies were spending a lot of money to come to America. And money was hard to earn in Eastern Europe.

This process was nothing like Ukraine Brides. There were many differences in the way the two businesses operated. The first thing I noticed was the way people met. There is no messaging or texting before the man and woman met in a video chat. During this chat, an Oksanalove.com matchmaker was on Skype to assist if necessary. In every case, the woman spoke some English. In some cases, she spoke good English and no translation was needed. This is important. If a woman had been on a site for years and has not learned fundamental English, she was not likely interested in leaving her country. The women on this site are serious.

I never understood how Oksana got the women to America. There are many types of visas. All of them are different and complicated. For example, a visa to get your spouse or child to America takes more than two years and is very expensive. Yet Oksana could get a large number of beautiful women to every love tour she hosted. I have asked her how she does this. She will talk to me about the process, but she doesn't directly answer my question because it's a business secret.

I don't know how many women are registered on the dating site. There are certainly hundreds. This all may sound complicated, but it isn't. I either waited for my matchmaker to inform me someone was interested in me, or until I was contacted directly by a lady. If I was contacted directly, I'd ask my matchmaker to arrange a Skype video chat, if I was interested. I had been on the site for a couple of months, and I was very well pleased with the results. I met some lovely ladies, and we discussed our meeting when they soon came to the U.S.

The tour was held in Sacramento, California. It sold out early. I was there.

Chapter Ninety-Six

I had several Skype video chats with women on Oksanalove.com. I regularly communicated with two who were in the U.S. and two who were in Russia. One of the women lived in Moscow. She was a very interesting 41-year-old lady who captured my attention immediately. She is smart and beautiful. She speaks good English. We met on Skype video several times and we communicated very effectively without a translator.

Tanya is a sophisticated Russian woman who is always busy. She has college degrees in Russian language and literature. She also has a law degree. I should also mention that she is a model and a television and movie actress. Tanya is well-read and we have discussions about books we have read. Coincidentally, one of my favorite books of all time is *The Brothers Karamazov*. The novel was written in the 19th century by the Russian writer Fyodor Dostoyevsky. Tanya thought it was incredible I had read this book. I think she thought I had read it in Russian. I immediately told her it was an English translation.

A few days after we began communicating, Tanya told me she wanted to meet me. She suggested we spend a week in Paris together. I was shocked. I could meet this woman in Western Europe. She said she could easily get a visa. She was anxious to meet as soon as possible. She suggested we begin making preparations for the trip. The very thought of the possibility of being near this incredible woman was all the motivation I needed.

When I told her about the one-bedroom apartment I had found on Airbnb with a view of the Eiffel Tower, she told me it was wonderful. The only suggestion she had was to change the one-bedroom apartment to a two-bedroom unit. She said the one-bedroom units were for spouses. I immediately thought of Mila. In fact, there is a striking resemblance.

I wanted to get something straight immediately. I told her intimacy was always the woman's decision, but I wasn't going to Paris, France with a beautiful woman if there was no chance of sex. She quickly told me she wasn't ruling out anything, and that was good enough for me.

At this point, I want to exercise a writer's prerogative and stop for an observation. Yes, I think it's that important.

I am convinced that Mila is a wonderful person. She had made important commitments she was determined to keep. No sex before marriage was one of those commitments. I completely understand that rationale. It is not a revolutionary or difficult concept. But I have some problems with the way Mila handled these issues.

First, she posted some provocative photos of herself on the Ukraine Brides website. Second, she wrote suggestive messages to me to encourage me to fly 6,000 miles to meet her. Then she wanted to discuss marriage before a single kiss was shared. I simply could not relate to that. I am not the least bit interested in a marriage without mutual attraction and affection. I never saw any affection in Mila. I think it would have made a lot of difference if she had just explained her decision about celibacy to me. She never said a word about her reasons. My point is that Tanya had handled her issue regarding intimacy very effectively and Mila had not.

Tanya had received her Western European visa, and we were making the final arrangements for our Paris trip. I hadn't been there in ten years, and I was excited about enjoying the great food and wine in the little bistros there. I looked forward to revisiting the Louvre and strolling along the Champs Elysees toward the Arc de Triomphe. I was also excited about meeting Tanya and seeing where it would go from there. It was my next big adventure. I was already brushing up on my limited French vocabulary. *C'est si bon!*

Chapter Ninety-Seven

Many will say, "Here we go again." Those are the nice people. Most are more graphic. I completely understand. My response is, "What are my choices?" Please don't recommend Walmart or Publix.

I am optimistic I will find a soulmate within the next twelve months. I believe there is a better than 75 percent chance she will not be from the U.S. I have dated more than thirty-five women in the past two and a half years. Only two of these relationships have developed into anything resembling long-term potential. Both of these have been with foreign women.

A friend recently told me, "Is dating all you do? You gave up golf, you sold your Harley, I don't see you at Chuck's Fish and you regularly turn down invitations for dinner with the guys. Man, you need to reengage with life."

I have been fortunate. I have made many mistakes in my life and most of these have been in the last couple of years. I know I have learned from these mistakes. I know I will be successful because I almost always have been. I know I will never give up because I don't know how. I believe I will find the woman of my dreams because I am giving it my very best effort, and when I do that, I almost always succeed.

Please don't follow my dating example. Feel free to live vicariously through my adventures, but do not try this at home. It is exactly like an amateur performing on the high wire without a net.

But feel free to hitch your wagon to my positive star, because that is the secret to my survival and my success. If you decide to do that, hang on, it's going to be one hell of a ride.

Yes, I traded for it. And it might not be the best deal in the world, but I am going to wrestle this son-of-a-bitch to the ground, and I will come out on top. There is no doubt in my mind.

I love you, dad. Can you hear me?

Epilogue

The road ahead is more important to me than the one left behind, but the two are inextricably linked. The road signs create a sense of excitement, but I can't help but think about the signs I misread.

I love clichés because their profound truths are so undeniable. These aren't mere theories, they are laws.

Two of my favorite clichés come to mind.

Insanity is doing the same thing over and over and expecting different results.

And…

Those who can't remember the past are condemned to repeat it.

As we age, our life expectancy increases simply because we have survived. We have survived because of our DNA and because of our propensity to make the right decisions most of the time. We decide to not smoke. We decide to exercise regularly, to eat a reasonably healthy diet, and to stay away from the edge of both literal and figurative cliffs. We know what helps us live a longer and more productive life, so we choose that lifestyle.

This doesn't mean we will always make the right choices. Notably, I find it much easier to avoid literal cliffs than the figurative variety.

In the end, my story had become much longer than I envisioned. I got bogged down in all the Oksana messaging. Later, I was delayed while licking my wounds.

My sentences were too long. So, I put my story aside for a while. My excuse was that I was waiting for a happy ending. I don't like stories with sad endings.

I am happy to report that Tanya and I had an incredible time in Paris. The apartment we agreed on was like a small museum. It was ancient. The elevator was claustrophobic. It was perfect. It had two bedrooms.

I wasn't sure at the time, but Tatiana (Russians have many names) and I had stumbled into a wonderful relationship. But I think we both saw the potential; because we were soon planning a meeting in Cancun, Mexico. Eventually, there would be five Cancun meetings. We ate great food, enjoyed the gorgeous beaches, and got to know each other. Our favorite place to eat in Cancun is a waterfront restaurant called Navios. It's located at kilometer marker 19.5 on Kukulcan Boulevard in the hotel district. There is not a more romantic place in Mexico.

We decided to get married at Navios. Westin Resorts handled everything for us down to champagne and the judge who officiated. We had gotten to know some of the staff at the restaurant and they were an important part of the wedding ceremony. A few friends came down from the states to join us. Tatiana was stunning in her white wedding dress. It was a perfect day.

Soon after our wedding, we applied for a spousal visa for Tatiana. The process took almost two years. Eventually, I decided to move to Moscow to wait for visa approval. It took nine more months. I damn near froze my ass off in what Tatiana described as the "warmest Moscow winter on record."

In March of 2020, Tatiana's visa was approved. We quickly boarded a plane from Moscow to London on British Airways, on the last day before the Domodedovo Airport was shut down due to the Covid virus. This airport is one of the busiest in the world and it was virtually abandoned. It reminded me of a Twilight Zone episode.

Recently, Tatiana beat me in a game of Scrabble. It was the English version. That's because she studies the English language every day. That's my story and I'm sticking to it. She loves America. She has her green card and will soon begin working on her citizenship. Then she will work on passing the bar so she can practice law in America. Tatiana and I are very much in love. I am finally home. And that's what I call a happy ending.

www.ingramcontent.com/pod-product-compliance
Lightning Source LLC
Chambersburg PA
CBHW041134110526
44590CB00027B/4011